McLuhan in Reverse

Lance Strate
General Editor

Vol. 8

───────────

The Understanding Media Ecology series is part
of the Peter Lang Media and Communication list.
Every volume is peer reviewed and meets
the highest quality standards for content and production.

───────────

PETER LANG
New York • Bern • Berlin
Brussels • Vienna • Oxford • Warsaw

Robert K. Logan

McLuhan in Reverse

His General Theory of Media (GToM)

PETER LANG
New York • Bern • Berlin
Brussels • Vienna • Oxford • Warsaw

Library of Congress Cataloging-in-Publication Data
Names: Logan, Robert K., author.
Title: McLuhan in reverse: his general theory of media (GToM) / Robert K. Logan.
Description: New York: Peter Lang, 2021.
Series: Understanding media ecology; vol. 8
ISSN 2374-7676 (print) | ISSN 2374-7684 (online)
Includes bibliographical references.
Identifiers: LCCN 2021010378 (print) | LCCN 2021010379 (ebook)
ISBN 978-1-4331-8245-7 (hardback) | ISBN 978-1-4331-8246-4 (paperback)
ISBN 978-1-4331-8247-1 (ebook pdf)
ISBN 978-1-4331-8248-8 (epub) | ISBN 978-1-4331-8249-5 (mobi)
Subjects: LCSH: Mass media—Philosophy. | McLuhan, Marshall, 1911–1980.
Classification: LCC P90 .L5844 2021 (print) | LCC P90 (ebook) |
DDC 302.23—dc23
LC record available at https://lccn.loc.gov/2021010378
LC ebook record available at https://lccn.loc.gov/2021010379
DOI 10.3726/b17321

Bibliographic information published by **Die Deutsche Nationalbibliothek.**
Die Deutsche Nationalbibliothek lists this publication in the "Deutsche
Nationalbibliografie"; detailed bibliographic data are available
on the Internet at http://dnb.d-nb.de/.

© 2021 Peter Lang Publishing, Inc., New York
80 Broad Street, 5th floor, New York, NY 10004
www.peterlang.com

All rights reserved.
Reprint or reproduction, even partially, in all forms such as microfilm,
xerography, microfiche, microcard, and offset strictly prohibited.

This book is dedicated to my family: Maria (Mana), Renee, Bruce, David, Natalie, Rebecca L., Paul, Haviva, Rebecca F., Jacob and Joshua

Table of Contents

Acknowledgments ix
Preface xi

Chapter One: McLuhan's General Theory of Media (GToM) and the Role of Reversals 1
Chapter Two: The Ten Elements of McLuhan's General Theory of Media 31
Chapter Three: Applying McLuhan's General Theory of Media to the Flowering of the Digital Age 87
Chapter Four: Understanding Humans: The Extensions of Digital Media 115
Chapter Five: General System Thinking and Marshall McLuhan's General Theory of Media 123
Chapter Six: Cataloguing McLuhan Reversals 139

Acknowledgments

I wish to acknowledge what I believe to be the source of my insight that reversals play a key role in McLuhan's GToM. Although I have been involved in McLuhan studies since 1974 when I first met Marshall McLuhan and began working with him, the insight that reversals played such a key role in his thinking is only a recent insight that is not more than a year or two old. I believe that what prompted this insight was the suggestion that Izabella Pruska-Oldenhoff made to me when she posited that there was a spiral structure to Marshall McLuhan's thinking. This led to a paper we wrote together entitled "The Spiral Structure of Marshall McLuhan's Thinking (Logan and Pruska-Oldenhoff 2017)." We further pursued this idea in a chapter in a book in press with Springer entitled *A Topology of the Mind*. The reason I wish to credit Pruska-Oldenhof's identification of the spiral structure of McLuhan's thinking with my insight of McLuhan's use of reversals is that the spiral structure contains the notion of reversal. As a spiral goes forward in one direction it reverses itself in the plane perpendicular to the forward motion going back and forth in a circular motion.

The original idea for Chapter Four was formulated as a direct result of listening to Douglas Rushkoff's presentation based on his book *Throwing Rocks at the Google Bus* at the McLuhan Centre for Culture and Technology at the University of Toronto on November 21, 2016. The idea was further developed as a result of the dialogue Doug and I had during his seminar presentation and in the private conversation that ensued after the seminar as well as the result of a number of email exchanges. The idea presented here that we become the content of digital media is basically Doug's with the exception of the twist I gave to it by suggesting the flip that we are extensions of the digital media we make use of instead of McLuhan's notion that our media are extensions of us, both of which are claimed to be true.

I wish to acknowledge the stimulating conversations of Philip Morais, JD candidate (Faculty of Law, University of Windsor) who asked me "What is the most important thing that Marshall McLuhan contributed?" My answer was the application of general systems thinking to the study of communications and the impact of technology and as a result of responding to Philip's question I eventually wrote Chapter Five of this book.

I also wish to acknowledge the editorial assistance I received from Callum Smith, B.A. in Communications (Royal Roads University in British Columbia).

Finally, I wish to thank the editor of Peter Lang's Understanding Media Ecology series, Lance Strate and the two reviewers, unknown to me, who reviewed my original manuscript. Their suggestions, in my opinion, led to a better book. Finally, thanks to the staff at Peter Lang especially Erika Hendrix and Ashita Shah for all their help and support. It is always a pleasure to work with Peter Lang, now the publisher of three of my books.

Preface

I first met Marshall McLuhan in 1974 at the Coach House on the campus of St. Michael's College, the University of Toronto. I was a professor of physics carrying out research in theoretical elementary particle physics, lecturing, supervising grad students, and from 1971 teaching in a seminar course, The Poetry of Physics and the Physics of Poetry. The objective of the seminar course was to introduce humanities students to physics without making use of mathematics (i.e. the poetry of physics) and integrating it with a study of poetry and other forms of literature that were related to physics (i.e. the physics of poetry). I started the course because I felt that too many bad decisions were being made by politicians and business people who had no basic understanding of science.

When I came up with the idea of the course I had no idea it would change my life, but it did because it became my ticket for meeting Marshall McLuhan and my subsequent collaboration with him. In 1974 after returning from spending three months studying and collaborating with Ivan Illich in Cuernavaca Mexico I organized a future studies seminar at New College known as the Club of Gnu. The name was a portmanteau of the New College mascot, the gnu and the Club of Rome, a prestigious NGO of futurists that had just commissioned the study The Limits to Growth. I recruited different professors to join the Club of Gnu from different departments in the University. Among them was Arthur Porter, the Chairman of the Industrial Engineering Department who I visited in his office.

He enthusiastically signed on to the project and immediately called his friend and colleague Marshall McLuhan asking him to join the Club of Gnu. When he mentioned my name, McLuhan asked "is that the Bob Logan who teaches the Poetry of Physics course?" Porter answered in the affirmative and McLuhan said send Logan over to the Coach House. I want to talk to him and invite him for lunch. And that conversation over lunch led to the start of my collaboration with Marshall McLuhan which lasted to his passing in 1980. During the six years I worked with Marshall I divided my time equally between working and publishing with him and pursuing my physics research. Once McLuhan was gone I decided to devote myself fully to carrying on his legacy publishing my last physics paper in 1982.

In the intervening years since I began working with McLuhan, I have been applying his insights into a number of different areas in addition to media ecology and McLuhan studies such as linguistics, education theory, systems biology, and cognitive science. Most recently, I suddenly had an insight and came to the conclusion that despite McLuhan's denial of not working from a theory that in fact his body of work constitutes what I will call his General Theory of Media (GToM). Furthermore, I also believe that McLuhan's GToM and his success in developing a revolutionary way of studying media and technology and their impacts is due to his use of reversals. In his study of media, he makes the following reversals:

(1) the usual emphasis on figure to that on ground;
(2) the emphasis on cause to that on effect;
(3) the emphasis on concept to that on percept; and
(4) the emphasis on content or the message to that on medium as in his famous one-liner "the medium is the message."
(5) in his Laws of Media (McLuhan 1975, 1977; McLuhan, M. and McLuhan, E. 1988) in which McLuhan asks what a medium i. enhances, ii. obsolesces, iii. retrieves and iv. reverses or flips into, he once again makes use of a reversal.

I have, therefore, concluded that McLuhan's body of work constitutes what I have called his General Theory of Media (GToM) and that the underlying theme of this theory is his use of reversals. This is the thesis that will be explored in this book. While McLuhan's famous Laws of Media are part of his GToM there are nine other elements of the GToM that I have identified. They are 1. his use of probes; 2. figure/ground analysis; 3. the idea that the medium is the message; 4. the subliminal nature of ground or environment revealed only by the creation of an anti-environment; 5. the reversal of cause and effect; 6. the importance of percept over concept and hence a focus on the human sensorium and media as extensions of man; 7. the division of communication into the oral, written, and electric ages along with the notions of acoustic and visual space; 8. the notion of the global village and finally, 9. media as environments and hence media ecology.

In developing McLuhan's GToM I want the reader to bear in mind that for McLuhan media are defined as any human artifact or any form of human technology and hence is not restricted to just communication media or technology but includes all forms of technology from the simplest hand tools and the human spoken language to automobiles, televisions and computers.

I realize that my approach of suggesting that McLuhan formulated a general theory of media runs counter to the way in which McLuhan's body of work is usually regarded.

The closest McLuhan came to considering a theoretical approach to his study of media came in his formulation of the Laws of Media which he referred to as the New Science, a term that Giambattista Vico used to describe his major philosophical work. McLuhan came to Vico through James Joyce. I suggest as a probe that the fourth law in McLuhan's Laws of Media, the law of reversal retrieves, Vico's notion of ricorso, the idea that history repeats itself. Vico used the term new science as he was critical of the way in which philosophy was following the analytic philosophy in the wake of Newton's mechanics. By the same token McLuhan was critical of the linear sequential thinking inspired by the alphabet and Newton's success with his mechanics, so he too thought of himself as creating a new science.

A hint that McLuhan saw the formulation of the Laws of Media as a form of science is the following remark found in his book with his son Eric, *Laws of Media: The New Science*: "Sir Karl Popper's (right brain) statement that a scientific law is one so stated as to be capable of falsification made it both possible and necessary to formulate the laws of media (McLuhan M. and McLuhan, E. 1988, 93)." The Laws of Media also known as a tetrad because of its four laws of Enhancement, Obsolescence, Retrieval and Reversal might also have been influenced by Aristotle four forms of cause: formal, efficient, material and final. McLuhan was interested in formal cause and wrote about it with his son Eric in a collection of essays entitled *Media and Formal Cause* (McLuhan M. & E. 2011).

In terms of scholars that have written about McLuhan I find some evidence that there was a scientific or scientific like approach in terms of systems theory to his scholarship and that of media ecology. I am not the first to *suggest a connection between McLuhan's* approach and emergence or systems thinking. Lance Strate (2006) also explores this connection and documents earlier attempts in this direction including my own earlier work when he wrote, "Systems concepts and approaches do appear in the media ecology literature over the past two decades (see, for example, Logan 2007; Rushkoff 1994, 2006; Strate 2006; Zingrone 2001)." Lance Strate (2017) returns to this theme in his book *Media Ecology: An Approach to Understanding the Human Condition*, as pointed out by his publisher, Peter Lang: "Strate provides an in-depth examination of media ecology's four key terms: medium …; bias …; effects, which are best understood via the Aristotelian notion of formal causality and **contemporary systems theory**; and environment (http://lancestrate.blogspot.com/2017/08/media-ecology-some-details-regarding-my.html, accessed May 30, 2020 [bolding mine])."

We shall deal in detail with the connection of McLuhan's GToM, media ecology and systems thinking in Chapter Five.

Paul Levinson (1999, 3) provides another link to the scientific basis of McLuhan's GToM in his book *Digital McLuhan* where he wrote, "In the scientific, and by extension social scientific, community, the surest way of determining to what extent someone's idea is right or wrong is to gauge the accuracy of its predictions." He then argues that what McLuhan wrote about the impacts of television cannot count as having made predictions because he lived through the television era. But that was not the case for McLuhan's predictions for the age of digital technology, an age he never lived long enough to experience. Hence according to Levinson, the accuracy of McLuhan's predictions that he, Levinson, documented in his book support the notion that there is a scientific dimension to McLuhan's theory of media. I will make the same argument in Chapter One in the section entitled: Predicting the Future: McLuhan's Prophecies That Have Come to Pass.

All said and done McLuhan was not a scientist, but he was an explorer. Perhaps it takes a scientist to see his work as constituting a General Theory of Media. I realize my hypothesis is unconventional but I ask the reader to play along with me to see another side of McLuhan's work. I have written this book in the spirit of McLuhan as a probe. And as he would often say even if it is only half true that is still a lot of truth. As I enter into the later stages of my run as a scholar I am willing to take a chance. But I believe that my approach, as unorthodox as it is, will provide you, the reader, with a new way to look at Marshall McLuhan's body of work.

So, let's explore this crazy idea of mine that Marshall McLuhan formulated a scientific theory of media and their effects. Let's begin by understanding the following terms scientific, science, theory and scientific theory. The word science derives from the Latin word scientia which in turn is derived from scire to know and came to be associated with knowledge, learning or a body of organized knowledge. This certainly fits the corpus of McLuhan's oeuvre as we will show in this study. As I once opined there was "method in his madness (Logan 2016, 19)." The word theory, on the other hand, is derived from the Greek word theorein meaning to look at, so both the word theory and theater are derived from the same Greek work, theorein. As the use and the meaning of the word evolved into Latin and modern European languages it came to mean contemplate or speculate, that is, a way of looking at things. The use of the word in the context of science itself came to mean "a coherent group of propositions formulated to explain a group of facts or phenomena in the natural world and repeatedly confirmed through experiment or observation" according to the definition of Dictionary.com (www.dictionary.com/browse/scientific-theory, accessed May 26, 2020). And as I will demonstrate, this definition describes McLuhan's GToM and hence his understanding of the effects of media, that is, all forms of technology, tools and human artifacts.

Now for those that need to be convinced more, let us consider Karl Popper's definition of a scientific proposition. According to him for a proposition to be scientific it must be falsifiable (Popper 1959). A number of McLuhan hypotheses had the potential to be falsified. For example, McLuhan's notion that a medium has effects independent of its content has the potential of being falsified but analyzes of different media have revealed that this is in fact the case. His hypothesis that we live in a global village has been borne out by the effects of the Internet which have been empirically verified by the fact that the Internet has recreated the nature of communication in a village where everyone knows everyone else's business. An empirical test of McLuhan theory that a medium has an effect independent of its content was the result of the 1960 Kennedy-Nixon debate that was both televised and broadcast over radio. People's perception of who won the debate depended on whether they viewed it on TV and listened to it on radio. "Americans who tuned in over radio believed the two candidates were evenly matched, but tended to think Nixon won the debates. But those 70 million who watched the candidates on television believed Kennedy was the clear victor (https://prologue.blogs.archives.gov/2010/11/15/does-television-affect-how-we-elect-presidents/, accessed May 26, 2020)."

This result clearly demonstrates that McLuhan's conjecture that a medium has an effect independent of its content since the content of the radio and TV broadcasts were the same. And it supports my notion that McLuhan had developed a scientific theory of the effects of media that made a prediction that could be verified with empirical data.

What the Reader Will Find

Chapter One – Does McLuhan's Body of Work Constitute a General Theory of Media? The argument is made that despite his claims to the contrary that

McLuhan's approach to understanding media and their effects was based on his General Theory of Media (GToM) that he never bothered to take the time to formulate.

In Chapter Two – McLuhan's General Theory of Media (GToM) is described in terms of the following 10 elements:

(1) probes;
(2) figure/ground;
(3) medium is the message;
(4) anti-environment reveals the subliminal nature of ground;
(5) the reversal of cause and effect among other reversals;
(6) the importance of percept over concept, the human sensorium and media as extensions of man (sic);
(7) the division of communication in the oral, written, and electric ages and the notions of acoustic and visual space;
(8) the Global Village;
(9) media as environments and media ecology and
(10) the Laws of Media.

In Chapter Three – Applying McLuhan's GToM to the Flowering of the Digital Age, the reversals of the digital era are described using McLuhan's GToM and his Laws of Media.

In Chapter Four – Understanding Humans: The Extensions of Digital Media, it is argued that in the digital age there is a reversal of McLuhan's media as extensions of man. Every keystroke that is made while using digital age Internet-based apps is captured by them and that data then becomes part of the app. As a result, there is a sense in which the human user becomes an extension of the app they are interacting with.

In Chapter Five – General System Thinking and Marshall McLuhan's General Theory of Media it is argued that the most important thing that Marshall McLuhan contributed was the application of general systems thinking to the study of communications and the impact of technology.

In Chapter Six – McLuhan Reversals, the reversals found in McLuhan's writings are catalogued as well as reversals for the digital age that have been formulated in the spirit of McLuhan reversals.

Reader Feedback

As I suggested above, I have written this book in the spirit of McLuhan as a probe and also as an exploration. I therefore welcome comments from my readers as to whether or not my probe has revealed for you any new aspect of McLuhan's work that you did not entertain before reading this book. I regard a scholarly book as a dialogue between the author and their readers. I therefore ask you to kindly sent me your comments by email to logan@physics.toronto.ca. I look forward to your communication and I will reply to all of your email posts.

CHAPTER ONE

McLuhan's General Theory of Media (GToM) and the Role of Reversals

Introduction

> Whenever provoked, Marshall McLuhan would declare, Look, I don't have a theory of communication. I don't use theories. I just watch what people do, what *you* do. Or words to that effect. That's the short answer to our question, "What is McLuhan's Theory of Communication?" (Eric McLuhan 2008)

Marshall McLuhan through his analysis of the effects of media ushered in a new way of looking at media and communications in what has become known as media ecology. He always claimed, as his son Eric just noted above, that he had no theory but that he merely observed what happened. "I don't explain, I explore," McLuhan (1967a) once exclaimed. I beg to differ with Marshall, who was my media ecology mentor. Yes, he observed like none other before him and yes, he explored, but he also explained and by the end of his career he formulated his famous four "laws of media (McLuhan 1975, 1977; McLuhan, M. and McLuhan, E. 1988)." The inclusion of "the new science" in the title of his book with son Eric: *The Laws of Media: The New Science* (ibid.) represents McLuhan's acknowledgment that there was a systematic, even a scientific way, in which he formulated his understanding of media and their impacts.

Well Marshall, if you formulated laws you must have had a theory. And since you refused to formulate your theory and were content with your four Laws of Media (LoM), I am going to formulate your General Theory of Media (GToM) for you with apologies and with respect making use of my training as a scientist and a physicist. In order to achieve the goal of formulating McLuhan's GToM I will make extensive use of his writings including his personal letters and things he said orally when being interviewed or giving a lecture. McLuhan's GToM is there in his writings and sayings and all I have done has been to re-assemble his words to provide his coherent theory of media and their effects/impacts. In a certain sense, the task I have assigned myself is as much editor as it is author. Having spent the last six years of Marshall's life collaborating with him, I believe I just might be qualified to achieve this task that I have set out for myself. I will share some of the things I heard him say which I have been unable to find in his writings or videos of his lectures or interviews. I will also share some anecdotes of my time working with Marshall to give the reader a sense of the man at the end of this chapter.

Some might suggest that the theoretical basis for McLuhan's treatment and understanding of media is contained in his world-famous aphorism, "the medium is the message," his notion of the Global Village and his division of human history in the three ages of oral, written and electrically configured information. While these are key element of what I have chosen to call McLuhan's General Theory of Media they do not encompass the richness of his thinking. The motivation for formulating McLuhan's GToM is to reveal this richness of his thinking, to provide a structure for his many observations and act as a guide for those who wish to practice media ecology, the field that his thinking and methodology gave rise to. The writing style I have adopted in this project is one that is straight forward and non-technical so as to also introduce McLuhan's thought for the non-specialist.

McLuhan's success in understanding media and his ability to predict so much of the developments of the digital age we live in is often attributed to McLuhan's brilliance, which is not to be denied, but there was a method to his brilliance, which I hope to reveal. He is recognized today as a genius who not only described the effects of technology and media of his day but who also predicted so much of the developments of the age of digital communication such as the Internet, the Web, social media, smartphones, AI and robotics. The successes he enjoyed were due not only to his genius but were also due to the systemic as opposed to systematic way in which he analyzed media and technology in which he adopted a field or ecological approach making use of a small number of principles or themes.

Electric Information, Figure/Ground and the Field/Ecological Approach

While "the medium is the message," the Global Village and the three ages of communication (oral, written and electric) were important elements of McLuhan's GToM, I want to suggest here that McLuhan's notions of reversals played a key role in his thinking and his GToM. In fact, I would suggest that the theme that seems to unite McLuhan's General Theory of Media (GToM) is that of reversals, which will be explored in this study. A few of the more prominent reversals include the reversal of figure and ground (where ground is the environment in which the figure operates), the reversal of cause and effect, the reversal of percepts and concepts, the reversal from the acoustic space of pre-literate oral communication to the visual space of writing and print and then the reversal back again from the written word to acoustic space, but this time of electrically configured information. For a full list of all of McLuhan's reversals see Chapter Six.

One of the images McLuhan used in his development of his analysis of media and their effects was the notion of the rearview mirror. "Most people … still cling to what I call the rearview-mirror view of their world (McLuhan 1969a)." In this study I will look at McLuhan's work through what I call the rearview lens to understand why reversals play such an important role in his GToM.

But why these reversals? Let's examine this. I would suggest that McLuhan's GToM and his focus on reversals can be traced back to his encounter with electric technology. They had a profound effect on his thinking about communications. Born in 1911, McLuhan was fascinated by electric technology. As a child Marshall built a crystal radio set that he would listen to with his brother Maurice. He enrolled in the University of Manitoba in engineering but then transferred to English in his second year at university. He once told me that during his first year at university he "read himself out of engineering and into literature." As a student of literary criticism, he recognized the profound changes that were created by the transition from an age of written communication to one of the electrically configured information with the telegraph, radio, movies, television and computers. I believe that McLuhan's analysis of the transformation brought about by electric based communication influenced many of his insights such as his field approach, which in turn helped him conceive of his figure/ground form of analysis. It also provided a stimulus for his use of reversals given the many reversals he observed from the patterns of pre-electric societies to the new patterns brought about by electrically configured information.

A hint of the influence of the transition from written to electric communication on McLuhan's analysis of media in terms of reversals comes from this passage in *Understanding Media* in which he writes:

> Today the great principle of classical physics and economics and political science, namely that of the divisibility of each process, has reversed itself by sheer extension into the unified field theory; and automation in industry replaces the divisibility of process with the organic interlacing of all functions in the complex. The electric tape succeeds the assembly line (McLuhan 1964, 48).

McLuhan observed the dramatic change from written information to electric information because of the almost instantaneous transmission of that information.

> My main theme is the extension of the nervous system in the electric age, and thus, the complete break with five thousand years of mechanical technology. This I state over and over again. I do not say whether it is a good or bad thing. To do so would be meaningless and arrogant (in a letter to Robert Fulford in 1964 Molinaro, McLuhan, C. & Toye 1987, 300).

> Unlike previous environmental changes, the electric media constitute a total and near-instantaneous transformation of culture, values and attitudes (McLuhan 1969a).

> Once it is understood that the hidden ground of our time is information moved at the speed of light, then it becomes easy to see why schooling is changing so drastically (Molinaro, McLuhan, C, and Toye 1987, 478).

This theme of the discontinuity between the age of the written word and the electric age laid the foundation for his figure/ground analyzes, his notion of a field or ecological approach as well as his many uses of reversals. McLuhan's understanding of the effects of electric media helped him develop his notion of figure and ground. He generalized the fact that electric media "create a total field of interacting events" so that every medium, every figure operates in that "total field of interacting events" which is the ground or environment of that medium or figure. The effects of electric media became for McLuhan a paradigm for his figure/ground analysis. I believe it also served as well as a paradigm for his many reversals given that he saw the literate age reverse back into the patterns of oral culture.

I will show that his notion that electric media gives rise naturally to a field perspective and hence negates the idea of a simple direct linear causal connection between a technology and its impacts. McLuhan adopted an ecological or environmental view of the interaction of media with each other and with their users. After all he was a media ecologist, perhaps the first, and although an ecological view incorporates causality, the relationships between the elements of a media ecology that includes the users and their technologies is not a simple one that can be summed up with a simple linear cause and effect form of technological determinism.

The reversal of patterns that McLuhan observed as his society transitioned from print to electric media became the foundation for his thinking about media and his incorporation of reversals into his GToM. For example, "the medium is the message" encompasses the reversal from an emphasis on the content of a medium to the effect of the medium independent of its content. Other reversals which form the backbone of McLuhan's GToM include:

- the reversal from a focus on figure to one on ground,
- the reversal from considering concepts to considering percepts,
- the reversal from starting with causes to starting with effects and
- the reversal from the visual space with written communication back to the acoustic space with electric media that also characterized oral communication.

I will explore each of these reversals and show how together they form McLuhan's GToM. There are many other examples of reversals in addition to the ones just mentioned that we will encounter as I describe McLuhan's methodology but I will leave these for later. Here we include a few, but as mentioned above, see Chapter Five for a complete list of McLuhan's reversals:

- the reversal from a medium pushed too far to a complementary or opposite form (from the Laws of Media);
- the reversal from the age of manufactured goods to the age of "do it yourself";
- the reversal from a work of art or performer to the public or audience, that is, "the user is the content";
- the reversal from jokes to grievances;
- the reversal from goal-seeking or job to role-playing;
- the reversal from centralism to decentralism with electric media;
- the reversal from specialism and expertise to interdisciplinarity;
- the reversal from linear sequential ordering of the mechanical literate age to an all at once or instantaneity of the electric age;

Why a General Theory of Media (GToM)?

Given that McLuhan claimed not to have a theory and given that "the medium is the message," the notion of the Global Village, the notion of the three ages of communication, oral, written and electric and the notion of acoustic space, the space of oral communication, versus visual space, the space of written communication, provide a great summary of McLuhan's approach to describing the effects of media, why the need to consider a general theory of media. I believe it is a useful exercise to have a framework with which to organize McLuhan's thoughts about media and their effects and hence this effort to formulate his General Theory of Media (GToM) characterized by his many reversals.

You might ask, how do I justify formulating McLuhan's body of work as a GToM. The first hint comes from the title of the book he wrote with his son Eric, *Laws of Media: The New Science* (McLuhan, M. and McLuhan, E. 1988). The last part of the title, The New Science, certainly suggests that there was a theory behind the laws. It is hard to imagine a science whether McLuhan's New Science or traditional science that could be formulated without a theory. After all science operates through the formulation of theories, which are tested by experiment and observation and are either confirmed, modified or discarded. The reader might ask why McLuhan used the term new science and what was its meaning.

Another hint that McLuhan (2005b, Vol. 19, 5) was thinking of his Laws of Media as a scientific hypothesis is this passage from the article "Laws of Media" in the McLuhan Unbound Project by Ginko: "When I came across Karl Popper's principle that a scientific hypothesis is one that capable of falsification, I decided to hypothesize the 'Laws of Media'." There we have it, McLuhan himself admitting his LoM were a scientific hypothesis. When McLuhan said, "I don't necessarily agree with everything I say," there is an explanation of how he could say he did not work from a theory and his statement above that he hypothesized the LoM as a scientific hypothesis.

I believe that what McLuhan meant when he claimed he didn't have a theory was that he worked strictly as an empiricist, as he said watching what people do and observing media and their effects on the psyche and the sensorium of their users as well as on the structures of society, their economic and political institutions, the work place, schools, universities, the family and just about any human activity that was mediated by the use of tools, technology or communication media. He started formulating his understanding of media by observing the effects on the percepts of the users of media and technology rather than with a theory of communication or a theory of media. This is why he claimed not to have a theory. He did not start with a theory but by working with observations in the end he actually developed a theory which I have labeled McLuhan's General Theory of Media (GToM).

McLuhan made no distinction between different kinds of human artifacts; they were all media whether they were a tool, a technology, a communications medium or even a scientific law or principle. He used the terms technology and media interchangeably. For him they were all media, where a medium is anything that mediates a person's interaction with their environment or surroundings. All media were according to McLuhan (1964) "extensions of man," which was the tag line of his ground-breaking book *Understanding Media: Extensions of Man* and they form a central part of McLuhan's General Theory of Media. For him communications media were extensions of our psyches and physical tools and technologies extensions of our bodies. I remind the reader that McLuhan's use of the term "man" would in today's parlance be translated into "humans" and "extensions of man" would translate into "extensions of humans." McLuhan wrote before it became politically incorrect to use the term "man" to refer to humankind.

As for why McLuhan never attempted to formulate his theory of media, we need to understand that he observed and analyzed first and foremost percepts and was less interested in concepts. Even in his religious thinking he claimed God was a percept and not a concept, something he told me on a number of occasions. Secondly, McLuhan was more acoustic than visual in his thinking and hence this is why he was more coherent when he spoke than when he wrote. He wrote to explore not to exposit and we are lucky to have the record of his thought processes, which is a treasure trove of ideas and insights.

McLuhan operated primarily in acoustic space, the home of percepts and not visual space, the home of concepts and theory. Theory is a conceptual entity that belongs to visual space. The word theory derives from the Greek word *theorein*, which literally means "to look at or see." The word theater has the same root. According to the Oxford English Dictionary the first use of the word "theory" in the English language is as follows:

> **1.** A sight, a spectacle. *Obs. rare.* 1605 L. Andrewes *96 Sermon: Passion* (1631) 365 Saint Luke … calleth the Passion θεωρίαν [theorian] a Theory or Sight … Of our blessed Saviour's whole life or death, there is no part but is a Theorie of it selfe, well worthie our looking on. The word theatre also is connected to the visual as this entry of the first and oldest use of theatre: **a.** *Ancient Greek Hist.* and *Roman Hist.* A place constructed in the open air, for viewing dramatic plays or other spectacles.

Acoustic and visual space are two key concepts of McLuhan's understanding of media which we need to understand because McLuhan's approach to studying media had an acoustic space bias. McLuhan used his notion of acoustic space to characterize pre-literate communication within the oral tradition. He contrasted acoustic space with space that characterized literate communication with writing especially alphabetic writing and then print. He suggested that the notion of "acoustic space" could also be used to describe the conveyance of electric information via telegraph, telephone, radio, television, and would certainly have added, and indeed embraced, the digital age that he so presciently foresaw. The idea of acoustic space is that information comes at you in all directions at once which is true for both spoken language and electronic information. Written communication, on the other hand, comes though the visual sense and it is perceived in a linear and sequential way, one thing at a time, that is, one word at a time and actually one letter at a time. It gives rise to the analytic and logical way of thinking characterized by scientific and mathematical thinking. McLuhan defined acoustic space as having its center everywhere and its margin nowhere (McLuhan and Wilfred Watson 1970, 39).

The advantage of McLuhan's working in acoustic space, which includes all the senses but sight, is that it places a greater emphasis on percepts versus concepts and hence it explores how media effect the human sensorium. Working in visual space with its connection to theory tends to focus on the ideas conveyed by a medium rather on their effects on the human sensorium independent of the ideas or content mediated by the medium. This is the new idea that McLuhan brought to the study of communications and media. It also expanded the field of the study of communications to include the effects of technology other than just communication technologies. As a result, media ecology also includes the study of the effects of the hammer, the plow, the steam engine, the automobile, etc. all of which are considered to be media just like the communication media of the spoken word, writing, the printing press, radio and TV.

McLuhan claimed he did not work from a theory and never formulated a theory other than his four Laws of Media that state that a human artifact (1) enhances some human function, (2) obsolesces a previous way of achieving that function, (3) retrieves something from the past that was obsolesced earlier and (4) when pushed to the limits of its potential reverses or flips into an opposite or a complementary form. Although, these Laws of Media are very insightful and useful, they do not incorporate the full scope of McLuhan's General Theory of Media (GToM), which is much richer than these four Laws of Media. The Laws of Media as we will see is only one element of what I have called has General Theory of Media. There are nine other elements of his GToM which we will encounter in Chapter Two.

The first hint that McLuhan's insights might constitute a general theory of media comes from a question framed by Tom Wolfe (1965): "*Suppose he is what he sounds like, the most important thinker since Newton, Darwin, Freud, Einstein, and Pavlov --- what if he is right?*"

Each of the scientist/scholars that Wolfe compares McLuhan to developed their own general theory of whatever it was that they were studying:

(1) For Newton it was his general theory of mechanics, motion and gravity.
(2) For Darwin it was his general theory of evolution and the origin of the species.
(3) For Freud it was his general theory of the role of the id, ego and super ego and the importance and impact of the unconscious and suppressed memories on the psyche.
(4) For Einstein it was his two theories of Special and General Relativity and the marriage of space and time.
(5) For Pavlov it was his general theory of conditioned reflexes and their effect on behavior and his contributions to physiology and neurology.

There is no better way to judge the validity of a scholar's contribution than to check whether his predictions came to pass. This is the basis of science. And on that account McLuhan is truly one of the great scholars/scientists and stands with Newton, Darwin, Freud, Einstein, and Pavlov as Tom Wolfe once suggested when he asked, "what if he is right?"

An early reader of this chapter and an avid McLuhan fan, Callum Smith, suggested that I add this comment which I have elected to share with my readers:

> As McLuhan tried vehemently, and while under constant scrutiny, jests, and laughter from an idiot public, to warn the world about their impending doom through his accurate predictions, he was as much a prophet as any in the Bible. He should therefore be classified with not just the usual modern thinkers such as Newton and Einstein, etc. but with Ezekiel, Jeremiah, and Isaiah, as well. Maybe you can incorporate that into your book. I believe that is plausible, and he deserves it!!! (private communication)

Not only is McLuhan a prophet according to Callum Smith, but for Wired magazine he is a saint, their patron saint.

Predicting the Future: McLuhan's Prophecies That Have Come to Pass

McLuhan brilliantly described the revolution that electricity and electric mass media had created in his own time. And as if that were not enough, he also prophesized and described the next revolution of digital media, a revolution he never had a chance to observe. He predicted or foreshadowed many of the developments of digital media and their effects on our way of life in the 21st Century. I will argue that there must have been a theoretical basis for his having made so many accurate predictions. He himself credited his ability to make predictions by understanding what was happening in the present. He famously said, "Everything that I predict about the future has already happened." But even if that is true why was he so far ahead of everyone else in describing the character of the digital age years before the Internet went public, years before the World Wide Web made its debut and years before the smartphone first appeared.

McLuhan developed his general theory of media just as Newton, Darwin, Freud, Einstein, and Pavlov developed their general theories before him. I claim that McLuhan had a general theory because of all the correct predictions and foreshadowings of the developments that characterize the digital media that he made 50 years before they finally surfaced and came to pass. In the next two sections I will describe all the predictions that McLuhan made and argue that he actually described our communications and technology era even better than his own. Finally, I will show that the charge that he was a technological determinist is without a basis in fact and that McLuhan's general theory represents a true breakthrough on a par with the scientists that Tom Wolfe compared him to. McLuhan, like them, also proceeded in his work through exploration, observation and pattern recognition rather than operating from a point of view.

So many of McLuhan's pronouncements about the effects of electric media are prophetic because it seems as though he was aware of the coming of personal computers, the Net, the Web and other digital media long before they arrived. Not only that, whatever McLuhan observed for electric media seems to apply even more so for digital media.

In 1959 20 years before personal computers and 35 years before the World Wide Web he already understood that the movement of information would dominate our economy when he wrote: "The production and the consumption of information ... is the main business of our time (McLuhan 2005a, 5)." He based this prediction on his knowledge of the effects of main frame computers that first appeared in the 1940s.

Although Marshall McLuhan never saw a personal computer during his lifetime, he predicted its arrival as his friend and colleague, Arthur Porter, related in the following reminiscence of a 1968 luncheon with McLuhan:

> Mac Hillock, [an IBMer] arranged a lunch with half a dozen of IBM's divisional directors. Marshall got soon tuned up and was telling them about a computer for every home [i.e. the personal computer], no need to visit the grocery store [i.e. Amazon for example] ... Two of them said to me after lunch, "we have not heard of anything as crazy as that!" Marshall was talking about the personal computer a dozen years before they thought of it. Here was a professor of English more than a decade ahead of the

technical people in computer evolution. He was thinking in terms of the user (Nevitt and McLuhan 1994, 29–30).

Another example of his prescience is that he, through his writing, also foreshadowed the Internet. William Gibson, the author *Neuromancer*, certainly deserves credit for coining the term cyberspace but long before *Neuromancer* was written or even conceived of, McLuhan (1967b, 67) described the Internet and the Web in the following passage in response to being asked, "How is the computer affecting education?" McLuhan's response was an almost exact description of the Internet and the Web:

> The computer in education is in a very tentative state but it does represent basically speeded up access to information and when it is applied to the telephone and to Xerox it permits access to the libraries of the world, almost immediately, without delay. And so, the immediate effect of the computer is to pull up the walls of the subjects and divisions of knowledge in favor of over-all field, total awareness–Gestalt.

McLuhan description of the Internet was complete if one reads telephone to represent packet switching over telephone lines and if one reads Xeroxing to represent the use of a printer. And he opined this description two full years before the development in 1969 of ARPANET, the forerunner of the Internet. An even earlier remark attributed to McLuhan in 1962 also foreshadows the Internet:

> A computer as a research and communication instrument could enhance retrieval, obsolesce mass library organization, retrieve individual encyclopedic function and flip into a private line to speedily tailored data of a saleable kind (http://en.wikipedia.org/wiki/Marshall_McLuhan).

One can also interpret without too much of a stretch the retrieval of "individual encyclopedic function" in the above quote as a foreshadowing of Wikipedia. One can also see a foreshadowing of Google if one interprets saleable data as the way Google generates advertising revenues from its searches.

In a 1967 address to an Ontario Provincial Committee on the Aims and Objectives of Education he wrote, "All the industries of our time are service industries. With Xerox the book becomes a service industry. It ceases to be a package or a product (McLuhan 1970)." This suggestion has become a reality but not through Xerox but another form of duplication, a digital one, namely, the e-book and services like the one that Amazon.com delivers with the Kindle. McLuhan also foresaw the transition from products to services as in many of today's Internet based services, namely, e-books, the downloading of software, cloud computing, iTunes and streaming services like Netflix.

During a TV interview in Toronto in 1966 McLuhan foreshadowed the notion of the Internet, Google, Amazon and the transition from products to services that now characterizes 21st century commerce (McLuhan 2005a, 101):

> Instead of going out and buying a packaged book of which there have been five thousand copies printed, you will go to the telephone [read Google and/or Amazon via the Net], describe your interests, your need, your problems, … and they say it will be right over. And they at once Xerox [read cut and paste], with the help of computers from libraries of the world, all the latest material just for you personally … They send you a package as a direct personal service. This is where we are heading under electronic information conditions. Products increasingly are becoming services.

McLuhan not only foreshadowed the Internet and Wikipedia, but he also foreshadowed crowd sourcing and Web sites like http://www.science2society.eu that connects researchers to solve problems from different disciplines and organizations in a process called "Open Innovation," which is described as follows:

> Open Innovation allows many people from different disciplines to tackle the same problem simultaneously and not sequentially. Anyone can participate with collaborative technology and Open Innovation training. When many minds are working on the same problem, it will take less time to solve it (www.science2society.eu/content/benefits-oi, accessed April 22, 2019).

Here is where McLuhan (1971) first described the idea of crowd sourcing, which he called "organized ignorance" in a convocation address at the University of Alberta:

> The immediate need and future of education is not in the dissemination of knowledge, but of ignorance. The open university of the U.K. made the ordinary mistake of putting the old curriculum and old classroom on the new T.V. media. The immediate need is for these media to bring, to the microphone and the studio, people from every field of knowledge and endeavor to explain to the public not their knowledge, but their ignorance; not their expertise, but their hang-ups; not their breakthroughs, but their breakdowns.

> The university and school of the future must be a means of total community participation, not in the consumption of available knowledge, but in the creation of completely unavailable insights. The overwhelming obstacle to such community participation in problem solving and research at the top levels, is the reluctance to admit, and to describe, in detail their difficulties and their ignorance. There is no kind of problem that baffles one or a dozen experts that cannot be solved at once by a million minds that are given a chance simultaneously to tackle a problem. The satisfaction of individual prestige, which we formerly derived from the possession of expertise, must now yield to the much greater satisfactions of dialogue and group discovery. The task yields to the task force.

McLuhan not only foreshadowed the development of the Internet, open source software development and crowd sourcing, but he with his co-author George B. Leonard in an article in the popular magazine *Look* also explained why the digital media would be so compelling to young people and to a certain degree their elders. They suggested that the age of print and the fragmentation that it encouraged was over. Here is another example of a reversal brought about by electrically configured information.

> More swiftly than we can realize, we are moving into an era dazzlingly different. Fragmentation, specialization and sameness will be replaced by wholeness, diversity and, above all, a deep involvement ... To be involved means to be drawn in, to interact. To go on interacting, the student must get some-where. In other words, the student and the learning environment (a person, a group of people, a book, a programmed course, an electronic learning console or whatever) must respond to each other in a pleasing and purposeful interplay. When a situation of involvement is set up, the student finds it hard to drag himself away (McLuhan and Leonard 1967).

He and Leonard also predicted that the relationship to humankind's knowledge would change with electrically configured information as we are beginning to see in this the Internet Age.

> When computers are properly used, in fact, they are almost certain to increase individual diversity. A worldwide network of computers will make all of mankind's factual knowledge available to students everywhere in a matter of minutes or seconds. Then, the human brain will not have to serve as a repository of specific facts, and the uses of memory will shift in the new education, breaking the timeworn, rigid chains of memory may have greater priority than forging new links. New materials may be learned just as were the great myths of past cultures-as fully integrated systems that resonate on several levels and share the qualities of poetry and song (ibid.).

Still another foreshadowing of McLuhan was that of the smart phone as described by his biographer Phillip Marchand (1989, 170).

> He told an audience in New York City shortly after the publication of *Understanding Media* that there might come a day when we would all have portable computers, about the size of a hearing aid [a hearing aid in his day was the size of today's smartphone], to help mesh our personal experiences with the experience of the great wired brain of the outer world.

He also foreshadowed eBooks and eReaders when he wrote in 1972, "When millions of volumes can be compressed in a matchbox it is not merely the book but the library that becomes portable (McLuhan 2005a, 175)." What makes this prediction even more amazing is that there were no personal computers at the time, no cell phones and no Internet (i.e. "the great wired brain of the outer world").

McLuhan's notion that the one-liner was the most efficient form of communication in the electric age foreshadows in our digital age texting, instant messaging and Twitter. McLuhan said, "We've invented the one-liner in place of the joke because people cannot wait around to hear you tell a joke … That's all we have time for. Attention span gets very weak at the speed of light (McLuhan 2005a, 271)." We have even less time in the digital age, so we have devolved the one-liner down to the 280-character Tweet not as a form of repartee or a joke but as the complete communication. If you cannot say whatever is on your mind in 280 characters forget it – I haven't the time; even an email is too long and as for a letter forget it.

Marchand (1989, 276) also pointed out McLuhan's (1964, 291) prediction in *Understanding Media* of the videocassette 20 years before its appearance and the streaming of videos on smartphones 35 years before its appearance when he wrote,

> At the present time, film is still in its manuscript phase, as it were; shortly it will, under TV pressure, go into its portable, accessible, printed-book phase. Soon everyone will be able to have a small, inexpensive film projector that plays an 8-mm sound cartridge as if on a TV to screen.

Let me suggest one more possible foreshadowing of McLuhan, namely that of the Web. Let me warn the reader that this is a sweeping generalization, which is at most half true but for a McLuhanite that's still enough truth to share it, at least as a probe. The book that McLuhan and Fiore (1967) co-authored, *The Medium is the Massage*, broke new ground in the way in which they integrated text and illustrations, as is the case with the Web. I would not claim that McLuhan predicted that the Web would emerge someday on the basis of the way text and images were combined in *The Medium is the Massage*, but I do believe in a certain sense he foreshadowed its development as I claimed earlier. It is interesting to note that the title of the book was intended to be *The Medium is the Message* but when they received the typesetter's proof set, they discovered that he had changed the title to *The Medium is the Massage*. McLuhan, who was a great fan of puns, liked the new title and decided to keep it and later explained his motivation for doing so, "the medium is the massage, not the message … it really works us over (McLuhan 2005a, 77)."

Given McLuhan's insights into how electric media would evolve one can hardly deny that McLuhan was a scholar of the highest order. It is clear that his insights were unique and that they were not matched by any other scholar of his generation whose focus was primarily on the analysis of the content of communication media and never considered to include media other than communication media such as clothing, housing, money, clocks, the wheel, bicycle, airplanes and motorcars all of which were analyzed in his ground-breaking book *Understanding*

Media (McLuhan 1964). Only those who discount his predictive powers and consider scholarship to be exposition of the known rather than the exploration of the unknown could suggest that his research was not revolutionary and that he was merely a technological determinist and a sloppy scholar. What McLuhan lacked in his inability to footnote his sources he made up for with his incredible insights.

Just as a footnote to his predictive powers I would claim that McLuhan even foreshadowed the concept of digital natives, a term that was coined in 2001 by Marc Prensky (See http://www.marcprensky.com/writing/Prensky%20-%20Digital%20Natives,%20Digital%20Immigrants%20-%20Part1.pdf accessed February 17, 2019). In 1958, over 60 years ago, McLuhan described the way in which youth and their parents would not speak the same language nor would they belong to the same culture. In the journal he co-edited with Ted Carpenter, *Exploration*, in Volume 8 he wrote, "Today the matrix of technology is releasing, not new vernaculars, but a whole series of new tongues, which the younger learn as mother tongues." He also suggested in the same article of what today we call attention economics: "The modern environment with its media carrying many messages simultaneously and at different levels demands new habits of attention."

McLuhan also described the kind of personalities that he thought would be successful in the age of electric technologies. "The future masters of technology will have to be light-hearted and intelligent (McLuhan 1969, 50)." This description fits the personalities of Steve Jobs and Steve Wozniak, the founders of Apple Inc., or the scientists at Xerox PARC that developed such things as the personal computer, the laser printer, the graphic user interface (GUI), the Ethernet, object-oriented programming, and ubiquitous computing. Today's masters of electric and digital technology are completely different than their industrial era counterparts. The heroes of 19th century Horatio Alger stories went from rags to riches through hard work, determination, courage, and honesty. Thomas Edison suggested that, "Success is 10 percent inspiration and 90 percent perspiration." The Silicon Valley tycoons are playful and in a certain sense are mavericks. Jobs and Wozniak started out as hackers who discovered a way to make long distance phone calls from pay phones for free.

McLuhan, back in the days when DIY strictly referred to do-it-yourself home improvement, foreshadowed today's digital DIY culture that includes such developments as indie music, hacking especially product hacking, grass roots politics and social activism. McLuhan wrote, "As technology advances, it reverses the characteristics of every situation again and again. The age of automation is going to be the age of 'do it yourself' (McLuhan 1995, 283)."

McLuhan also foreshadowed the idea of product hacking and remixing when he introduced his notion that hybridization releases energies and creates new forms: "It is from such intensive hybrid exchange and strife of ideas and forms that the greatest social energies are released, and from which arise the greatest technologies (McLuhan 1964, 56)." "The hybrid or the meeting of two media is a moment of truth and revelation from which new form is born (ibid., 63)."

The last quote is a perfect description of the impact of the smart phone and the tablet, both of which are hybrids of many different technologies that the digital format makes possible. The smart phone is an Internet terminal, a camera, a texting device, a television receiver, a player of recorded music and also, by the way, a telephone for voice communication.

McLuhan's understanding of the power of hybridization supports the hypothesis that McLuhan, in a certain sense, foreshadowed the notion of emergence. The creation of new form and the release of new energies with hybridization echoes the notion of emergence and the idea that the whole is greater than the sum of the parts in which properties not possessed by the components of the hybrid system emerge through the hybridization process.

In addition to his piercing analyzes of the events and trends of his day and his many foreshadowing and predictions of our times, McLuhan also led an assault on the specialism of his times and blazed a trail that has made the inter- and multi-disciplinary approach to scholarship acceptable and, more and more, the norm.

The False Charge of Technological Determinism

Those who would argue against my suggestion that McLuhan developed a general theory of media would be those who accused him of technological determinism as a way to dismiss his work that contradicted their own approach to analyzing media. First of all, the charge of technological determinism is not the worst thing on can say about someone's work. Weren't Newton, Faraday, Maxwell, Einstein, Darwin and Pavlov determinists and isn't determinism at the heart of explanatory science. All formulators of scientific laws are determinist. Even quantum mechanics, which gives up on causality at the micro-atomic level for individual particles, retains it for predicting the behavior of large ensembles of particles. It is this level of determinism that has led to our understanding of the solid-state physics that makes today's digital technology possible.

The charge of technological determinism in the pejorative sense is without foundation when one considers that McLuhan adopted a field or ecological approach to explaining the interactions and impacts of media and never suggested a one to one correspondence between an effect and a cause. Of course, if one wishes to label anyone who posits a mere relationship between technology and societal transformation as a technological determinist then McLuhan is guilty. Anyone one who would deny a relationship between technology and societal transformation would be hopelessly naïve and out of touch with social realities. Yes, McLuhan asserted that technology impacted society but he never suggested it was the sole factor. Clearly McLuhan was not a single cause explainer of anything. He railed against the notion of the "point of view" and the "single vision of Newton." He described an insight as "the sudden awareness of a complex process of interaction," which is how he regarded the relationship between media and society.

He once said, "we live today in the Age of Information and Communication because electric media instantly and constantly create a total field of interacting events in which all men participate" (McLuhan 1964, 248). A field approach rejects the notion of a linear cause and effect model, which characterizes naïve "technological determinism." And finally, he often talked about the reversal of cause and effect so how could he be accused of being a technological determinist – it doesn't make sense. Having dismissed the charge of technological determinism let's look at McLuhan's framework for understanding media and their effects, namely, his General Theory of Media.

The Posthumous Formulation of McLuhan's General Theory of Media (GToM)

The first thing I need to make clear to the reader is that McLuhan never formulated a theory of media and in fact as I have already mentioned he actually claimed not to work from theory at all. So, this formulation of McLuhan's GToM is my synthesis of his observations, explorations, probes, and comments based on both his written and oral pronouncements. Perhaps he was too close to his own work to have realized that he had in fact formulated a general theory of media. The other possibility is that he was too busy formulating the different aspects of his general theory of media to take the time to sum up his work and formulate it as a theory of media. He did take the time to formulate his four Laws of Media, which are an important element of his GToM but in and of themselves do not encompass the richness of his ideas or the totality of his theory.

Another explanation of why McLuhan never formulated his ideas as a theory is that he worked more in the oral tradition than in the written one. He wrote, "I do a lot of my serious work while I'm talking out loud to people. I'm feeling around, not making pronouncements. Most people use speech as a result of thought, but I use it as the process." Scientists also need to discuss their ideas with each other but not to the same extent as McLuhan did.

His writings were basically a mosaic of his observations rather than a carefully developed narrative with a beginning, a middle and an end. Given McLuhan style of writing the formulation of a theory would be difficult. There is also his premature incapacitation at age 68 from a stroke and his death at age 69 that might have closed the door on such a project. Finally, it is only with the emergence of digital media and their effects that one realizes the depth of his thinking and the ability of his analysis to provide a roadmap of the future of media. His General Theory of Media was not a post hoc description of what was already known to him but rather it was a description of things to come, which is the mark of a grand theory like those of Newton, Darwin, Freud, Einstein, and Pavlov. Like them he made predictions that came true.

Justification for Regarding McLuhan's Methodology as a Theory Given that He Claimed Otherwise and Repeatedly Claimed not to have a "Point of View" or a Theory

McLuhan's interest in science led directly to his empirical style of scholarship based on direct observation and exploration. Unlike many academics, he did not start from a point of view but kept his mind open to new possibilities. He also mined the scientific literature to develop his unique use of the field concept and the resonant interval that led directly to his notion of acoustic space for both preliterate oral communication and electrically configured information. He contrasted these with the visual space of literary culture.

McLuhan acknowledged he did not have a "point of view." But this does not preclude him developing a new theory. Many scientists also started their research with no point of view. If Einstein had a Newtonian point of view, he would not have developed his theory of relativity. If Bohr had started with a Newtonian point of view, he would not have developed his complementarity principle, which led to the subsequent development of quantum mechanics. Thomas Kuhn (1962) is his book *The Structure of Scientific Revolutions* made a distinction between normal science and revolutionary science. In normal science a scientist works from an existing paradigm to enrich an existing scientific point of view. In revolutionary science, a scientist creates a new paradigm which becomes the basis for a new point of view. Einstein and Bohr are examples of scientists who created new paradigms. I believe what McLuhan was saying when he claimed to have no point of view was that he was developing a new paradigm and hence did not work from the point of view from some existing paradigm.

In pursuing his scholarship McLuhan operated more out of the acoustic space of the oral tradition rather than the traditional literary visual space. A distinguishing characteristic of McLuhan's program of exploration is the absence of the traditional methodology of orthodox scholarship whereby a particular "point of view" or hypothesis is articulated and all subsequent observations are made to support or refute it. McLuhan described his approach of working without a "point of view" as "observation minus ideas" (McLuhan 1977). A point of view is characteristic of visual space and ties one down to a single perspective and limits the richness of the insights that one can develop. A point of view represents the visual bias of the written word rather than the simultaneous, all-at-once, acoustic flow of information characteristic of both the electric information age and the oral tradition (Logan 2013, 64).

Working without a point of view allows one to create a new perspective or a new paradigm and hence a new theory or, if you will, a new point of view. So, I would claim that McLuhan did not work from a former point of view but as a result of making a fresh start arrived at his GToM, which is actually a new point of view.

In the spirit of McLuhan's enjoying the give and take of a spirited discussion especially if it contained a paradox or an element of humor, I will suggest that his claim to not having a point of view was in itself a point of view.

The point-of-view approach leads to classification, whereas working with interface leads to pattern recognition. The point-of-view approach corresponds to what Thomas Kuhn calls "normal science" (Kuhn 1972). Once a revolutionary idea succeeds in describing a new set of data or phenomena, a new paradigm develops, which is imitated and articulated in as many areas of application as possible. The development of a new paradigm is "revolutionary science" and requires the lack of a point of view. "Normal science," or the articulation of the new paradigm, involves the adoption of the new paradigm as a point of view. McLuhan operated throughout his career in the revolutionary mode without a particular point of view or paradigm. The scientist engaged in revolutionary science becomes the target of critics, who are proponents of the older point of view, that is, the paradigm that is being replaced by the new revolutionary paradigm. This explains the viciousness and vitriolics of many of McLuhan's critics who saw their old paradigm being swept away by this light-hearted professor who did not observe the decorum of specialized academic life.

McLuhan (Innis 1972) acknowledged his debt to Harold Innis when he wrote that Innis was the giant upon whose shoulders, he stood in his Introduction to the 1972 edition of Innis's book *The Bias of Communication*, originally published in 1950. He also claimed in that Introduction that Innis had no point of view. McLuhan wrote,

> He (Innis) changed his procedure from working with a 'point of view' to that of the generating of insights by the method of 'interface.' By contrast, a 'point of view' is merely a way of looking at something. But an insight is the sudden awareness of a complex process of interaction (ibid., viii).

I therefore claim that what McLuhan was suggesting that what he and Innis were doing by not working from a point of view was that they were developing a new paradigm in the Kuhnian sense. I further claim that McLuhan's claim not to work from a point of view does not preclude him having developed a General Theory of Media.

In a letter to William Kuhns dated December 6, 1971 McLuhan claimed "I have no theories whatever about anything. I make observations by way of discovering contours, lines of force and pressures (Molinaro, McLuhan C., and Toye 1987, 448)."

If we look at his remark "I have no theories whatever about anything" in the full context of his remark in his letter to Kuhns we will see that he actually contradicts himself.

> I have no theories whatever about anything. I make observations by way of discovering contours, lines of force and pressures. I satirize at all times and my hyperboles are as nothing compared to the events to which they refer. If you study symbolism you will discover that it is a technique of rip-off by which figures are deliberately deprived of their ground. You do not seem to have grasped that the message as it relates to the medium, is never the content, but the corporate effects of the medium as an environment of service and disservice (ibid.).

In the very last sentence, he actually partially articulates his theory that the "message" or "effect" is not in the figure of the content but in the ground or environment of the medium, that is, "the medium is the message."

If what McLuhan said was true that he had no theory and that he was only describing what he observed how do we explain his ability to make the many successful predictions he made, even the prediction of the emergence of personal computers that the IBM executives thought was crazy. No, I must disagree with my mentor. Predictions, especially the large number that McLuhan made successfully can only emerge from a theoretical foundation. As noted earlier, the word theory derives from the Greek word theorein to see or look at. McLuhan was able to look at or see the contours of the digital age years before they finally emerged. This could only have been done within a theoretical context. As I mentioned early the roots of the word theory comes from the Greek word *theorein*, which literally means "to look at or see" and hence to look at or see, (theorein) the future requires a theory.

The consideration of figure and ground and their reversal is at the heart of McLuhan's GToM. It was the concept from which his various insights emerged. Although "the medium is the message" and the notion of the global village are better known than the figure/ground dichotomy it is the latter that fueled McLuhan's analysis of media and provided him with the insights to see the contours of the digital information age years before they emerged.

I opened this section with a quote from Marshall McLuhan's son in which he claimed his father said, "I don't have a theory of communication. I don't use theories. I just watch what people do (Eric McLuhan 2008)." But I have a found place where McLuhan has actually claimed to have developed some sort of theory. In a lecture he gave at the University of Southern Florida in 1970 that was videoed he talks about Shannon's Information Theory and his own theory:

> All the official theories of communication studied in the schools of North America are theories of how you move data from point A to point B to point C with minimal distortion. That is not what I study at all. Information theory I understand, and I use, but information theory is a theory of transportation, and it has nothing to do with the effects which these forms have on you. It's like a railway train concerned with moving goods along a track. The track may be blocked, may be interfered with. The problem in the transportation theory of communication is to get the noise, get the interference off the track and let it go through. Many educators think that the problem in education is just to get the information through, get it past the barrier, the opposition of the young, just to move it and keep it going. I don't have much interest in that theory. **My theory** or concern is what these media do to the people who use them. What did writing do to the people who invented it and used it? What do the other media of our time do to the people who use them? **Mine is a transformation theory**, how people are changed by the instruments they employ (www.marshallmcluhanspeaks.com/media/mcluhan_pdf_6_JUkCEo0.pdf, accessed April 27, 2019).

There are other places where McLuhan hints at the possibility of a theory of culture change or a theory of communication. In *Gutenberg Galaxy*, McLuhan (1962, 49) wrote, "a theory of cultural change is impossible without knowledge of the changing sense ratios effected by various externalizations of our senses." In *The Book of Probes* (McLuhan and Carson 2003, 362) he wrote, "without an understanding of causality there can be no theory of communication. What passes as information theory today is not communication at all, but merely transportation." McLuhan does not suggest that he was developing a theory of communication but given his critique of the work of others who else, but he, would be capable of producing a theory of culture change or communication. Based on these two remarks and the one quoted above from his 1970 lecture I conclude that McLuhan had an ambiguous attitude towards theory and that towards the end of his career he was entertaining the idea of a possible theory of media or communication. Hence, his Laws of Media.

McLuhan published his two papers on the Laws of Media (McLuhan 1975, 1977) in 1975 and 1977. During this time frame and up to the time in 1979 when McLuhan suffered the stroke that incapacitated him, he was actively working on the Laws of Media. He and I worked on the Laws of Media for physics. The LoMs that we developed linked Aristotle's physics, Buridan's notion of impetus, Newton three laws of motion and Einstein's theory of relativity appeared in *Laws of Media: The New Science* (McLuhan M. and McLuhan E. 1988, 212–14) that his son subsequently published. While this is only speculation, I believe that he was entertaining the notion of a systematic theory of media based on our conversation while working on the LoMs. I also believe that his disavowing of not having a theory was his way of critiquing the theoretical frameworks of other scholars working in the field of media and communications especially that of Shannon, which others referred to as information theory but which he labeled as a "theory of transportation."

What McLuhan Was Trying to Achieve with his GToM

McLuhan (1969) wrote, "Today, in the electronic age of instantaneous communication, I believe that our survival, and at the very least our comfort and happiness, is predicated on understanding the nature of our new environment." This quote illustrates McLuhan's concern with the effects that technology have on us. "McLuhan was not just a scholar – he was also a social critic, a social reformer, a futurist, and an educator. One might even say a humorist Louis Forsdale (1988, 175)."

Before describing McLuhan's GToM we should first consider what was he trying to achieve with his research. Like all scientists or scholars McLuhan was trying to achieve a better understanding of the world in which he lived. But in addition to this he had a specific goal which he expressed in the following three quotes: "The central purpose of all my work is to convey this message, that by understanding media as they extend man, we gain a measure of control over them (McLuhan 1969)." "I am in the position of Louis Pasteur telling doctors that their greatest enemy was quite invisible, and quite unrecognized by them (McLuhan, 1964, 18)." "Is it not possible to emancipate ourselves from the subliminal operation of our own technologies? Is not the essence of education civil defense against media fallout? (McLuhan 1962, 294)."

In addition to understanding his world like any other scientist/scholar McLuhan was also a social critic trying to get his society to gain control of their technology before it gained control of them. He hoped to do this by getting us to understand the subliminal effects of technology and not just the purposes we use them for. This is why he likened himself to Louis Pasteur, who also battled an unseen force.

The fact that he was trying to understand the impacts of technology and media to benefit humankind does not preclude him from being a scientist or developing a scientific theory. Scientist also try to understand nature to be able to control it and harness it for the benefit of humankind.

The Ground of McLuhan's Thinking and His GToM

Before describing McLuhan's GToM let us first examine the various influences on McLuhan's thinking that led to his GToM. As we will soon discover that the distinction between a figure and the ground in which it operates is the key to understanding McLuhan's approach to understanding media. It is therefore prudent to have a cursory look at the ground in which McLuhan was operating by identifying the scholars, scientist and artists that influenced his thinking.

McLuhan drew on the ideas of many scholars and synthesized their insights. What was unique about McLuhan was that he put together all of their ideas together with his own to create a coherent general theory of media and their effects. Those social scientists and philosophers that influenced him (with their area of expertise and what they contributed to his theory in parentheses) are:

- Aristotle (contributed the notion of formal cause)
- Kenneth Boulding (systems thinker and economist),
- Edmund Carpenter (anthropology contributed insights into oral culture),
- W. T. (Tom) Easterbrook (political economy),
- G. K. Chesterton (philosophy contributed to McLuhan's religious thinking)

- **Jacques Ellul (sociologist),**

- Sigmund Freud (psychiatrist contributed the notion of the unconscious),
- Sigfried Giedion (art historian),
- Ernst Gombrich (art historian),
- Siegfried Giedion (historian of architecture contributed impact of technology),
- Edward T. Hall (anthropology),
- Eric Havelock (classics scholar contributed importance of oral culture and the tribal encyclopedia),

- Ivan Illich (futurist and education critic)
- Harold Innis (political economist and systems thinker contributed writing on durable media gives control over time and writing on papyrus gives control over space; monopolies of knowledge and media as staples),
- F. R. Leavis (the new criticism),
- Albert Lord (oral culture scholar contributed insights into oral culture),
- Lewis Mumford (sociologist specialized on the impact and critique of technology),
- Walter Ong (media ecologist contributed insights into oral culture, the impact of the printing press and Ramism),
- I. A. Richards (literary critic contributed the notion of feedforward and hence the reversal of cause and effect),
- Milman Parry (oral culture scholar contributed insights into oral culture),
- Teilhard de Chardin (theologian contributed the notion of the noosphere),
- Jacqueline Tyrwhitt (urban studies scholar),
- Giambattista Vico (philosophy contributed the idea of the New Science which McLuhan used as the sub-title for the Laws of Media book as well as his criticism of Newton's single vision),
- Lynn White (historian specialized on the impact of medieval technology) and
- Carl Williams (psychologist contributed the notion of acoustic space).

In addition to the media scholars just listed, McLuhan was also influenced by the following artists and scientists, whose ideas he integrated into his analysis of media. Among the artists and writers were

- T. S. Eliot,
- James Joyce (the power of the pun),
- Wyndham Lewis (who provided him with the notion of artists as antennae of the race),
- Edgar Allan Poe (descent into the Maelstrom),
- Ezra Pound,
- the Symbolist poets (where he picked up the notion of synesthesia, the sensorium and the primacy of percept over concept),
- the impressionist and cubist painters.

Among the scientists and cyberneticists were

- Gregory Bateson, ecologist (systems thinking),
- Ludwig von Bertalanffy, biologist and cybernetician (systems thinking),
- The quantum physicists Niels Bohr, Linus Pauling, Louis de Broglie, and, in particular Werner Heisenberg from whom McLuhan borrowed the concept of the resonant intervals (Elena Lamberti 2012, 92),

- Albert Einstein and the theory of relativity from which McLuhan developed the notion of the speed up of information moving at the speed of light,
- Buckminster Fuller (cyberneticist contributed the notion of technology as extensions of the body),
- gestalt psychologists and their notion of figure/ground,
- Hans Selye, endocrinologist (impact of stress and trauma on the human psyche),
- Claude Shannon, information theorist
- Norbert Wiener, mathematician (cybernetics).

These scientists provided McLuhan with the scientific concepts of electricity, fields, systems thinking, quantum mechanics, Einsteinian relativity, biological ecology and stress that he made frequent use of in his analysis and understanding of media and their effects.

McLuhan's General Theory of Media: An Amalgamation

McLuhan, unlike any scholar before him, pioneered a multidisciplinary and a general systems approach to the study of media, literature, art, culture, education, work and society as the list of scholars, artists and scientists who influenced him indicates. A key aspect of his approach was the use of the probe, which is the formulation of a hypothesis to see where it would lead. It is a form of abduction. This is a standard practice in science where hypotheses are formulated that have to have the possibility of being falsifiable. McLuhan was willing to explore ideas that might be valid or might not but as in science even a negative result has some value. When he formulated a probe, he was not always sure that it was correct, but he believed it would lead to some insight whether or not it was correct. That was the spirit of the journal *Explorations in the Study of Culture and Communication* that he and Edmund Carpenter launched and co-edited in 1953 and ran until 1972. In the mission statement of the journal Carpenter and McLuhan (1953) wrote: "*Explorations* is designed not as a permanent reference journal that embalms truth for posterity, but as a publication that explores and searches and questions." A revival of *Explorations* entitled *New Exploration* was launched in May of 2020 and can be found at https://jps.library.utoronto.ca/index.php/nexj/index with information that allows the reader to access back issues of the original *Explorations* journal.

McLuhan's probing and his approach to understanding media and what I have identified as his General Theory of Media has a number of elements that made his approach to studying media unique. McLuhan with his thorough grounding in literature and the arts and his uncanny ability to grasp the ideas of science and the social sciences created an amalgam of ideas unlike that of any scholar of media, communications and culture before him. In the next chapter we will examine the ten elements that make up McLuhan's general Theory of Media and how they are intertwined, but before moving to Chapter Two I will close this chapter with an account of what it was like to collaborate with Marshall McLuhan.

Co-authoring with Marshall McLuhan

To give the reader some sense of how McLuhan worked and how he collaborated with others I am going to share with the readers an excerpt from my book McLuhan Misunderstood: Setting the Record Straight (Logan 2013, 40–43) which describes how my collaboration with McLuhan began and how our paper Alphabet, Mother of Invention (McLuhan and Logan 1977) came into being. As one of the last living collaborators of Marshall McLuhan I thought it might prove useful to the reader to learn how McLuhan probed ideas and how he collaborated with others. I want to thank Ed Tywoniak, an emeritus professor of media ecology at St. Mary's College in California with whom I consulted on this project for encouraging me to include this section in my book.

An excerpt from *McLuhan Misunderstood: Setting the Record Straight* (Logan 2013)

Having co-authored two published articles with Marshall (McLuhan and Logan 1977, 1979) and the book *The Future of the Library an Old Figure in a New Ground* (Logan and McLuhan 2016) I can provide some insight of how he worked with one collaborator, namely me. Our first article together grew out of a conversation we had the very first day that I met Marshall McLuhan. I was organizing a seminar, The Club of Gnu, on future studies at New College, University of Toronto in 1974 and recruited Prof. Arthur Porter, the Chair of the Industrial Engineering Department. He called Marshall to invite him to join our seminar and mentioned my name. McLuhan had heard about my course the Poetry of Physics and the Physics of Poetry and instructed Porter to send me over to the coach house to have lunch with him. I was very excited to be having lunch with such a famous scholar and a celebrity to boot.

We lunched at the faculty cafeteria at St. Michael's College and as soon as we sat down with our trays McLuhan immediately asked me what I had learned by teaching the Poetry of Physics. I explain that I was fascinated by the problem posed by Joseph Needham (1956) in his book the *Grand Titration* of why abstract science began in the West despite the fact that so much of technology originated in China. I proposed that since monotheism and codified law were unique to the West and that together they gave rise to a notion of universal law that this might explain the Needham paradox. Marshall McLuhan nodded his head in agreement and then asked me pointedly what else did we have in the West that was not present in China. I was totally intimidated by McLuhan who seemed to be talking to me at 100 miles per hour. I was unable to think and finally I said, "I give up." He smiled and said, "the alphabet, of course."

I let out the loudest groan because I immediately saw where he was going as I recalled that he had showed the connection of the alphabet with abstract science and deductive logic in *The Gutenberg Galaxy* (McLuhan 1962) and *Understanding Media* (McLuhan 1964). It all became so obvious – the alphabet serves as a model for analysis, classification, coding and decoding. To use the alphabet to write one must analyze each word into its basic phonemes and then represent each phoneme with a meaningless visual sign, a letter of the alphabet. So, writing with an alphabet is coding sounds into visual signs and reading an alphabetic text is decoding the visual signs back into sounds. As far as classification goes the alphabet allows every word and every name to be ordered alphabetically as is the case in a dictionary. The alphabet is totally abstract as there is no connection between the letters representing the word and what the word represents which is not the case with pictographs, ideograms or Chinese characters.

Taken altogether the alphabet promotes abstraction, codification, classification and analysis the basic skills needed for abstract science and deductive logic. Realizing that our independent explanations for the rise of abstract science in the West complemented and reinforced each other, we combined our ideas and developed the hypothesis that the phonetic alphabet, codified law, monotheism, abstract science and deductive logic were ideas unique to the West originally and that they reinforced each other's development.

All of these innovations, including the alphabet, arose within the very narrow geographic zone between the Tigris-Euphrates river system and the Aegean Sea, and within the very narrow time frame between 2000 B.C. and 500 B.C. We did not consider this to be an accident. While not suggesting a direct causal connection between the alphabet and the other innovations, we would claim, however, that the phonetic alphabet (or phonetic syllabaries) played a particularly dynamic role within this constellation of events and provided the ground or framework for the mutual development of these innovations.

The effects of the alphabet and the abstract, logical, systematic thought that it encouraged explain why science began in the West and not the East, despite the much greater technological sophistication of the Chinese, the inventors of metallurgy, irrigation systems, animal harnesses, paper, ink, printing, movable type, gunpowder, rockets, porcelain, and silk. Credit must also be given to monotheism and codified law for the role they played in developing the notion of universality, an essential building block of science. Almost all of the early scientists, Thales, Anaximander, Anaximenes, Anaxagoras and Heraclitus, were both lawmakers in their community and monotheistically inclined. They each believed that a unifying principle ruled the universe.

Right then and there at our first meeting in the faculty cafeteria we decided to write up these ideas and publish them as a research article. During this whole conversation I was taking notes. McLuhan was only talking. At a certain point in our discussion he said to me please write up these ideas and we can discuss them further. As soon as I left that luncheon I went home and wrote up the ideas we had discussed. I remember being very nervous because I was not sure how McLuhan would take to the notion that the phonetic alphabet had helped the Hebrews to conceive of the notion of monotheism and the existence of God. I was worried this might offend McLuhan's Roman Catholic sensibilities. I needn't have worried. He was fine with the idea and basically accepted the paper largely as I had written it. As I read it to him the next day while he lay on his couch or day bed, he would ask me to change a phrase here and a word there. He amplified a couple of points that were being made in the paper but basically accepted the document as I had read it to him. He also suggested the title, Alphabet, Mother of Invention (McLuhan and Logan 1977).

Once he was finished making his suggestions he asked me to give the handwritten manuscript with his additions to his secretary Marg Stewart to be typed up. He sent the paper to Neil Postman, who was the editor of Etcetera, the journal of the International Society of General Semantics. The paper was accepted after being reviewed by Paul Levinson, a grad student at the time. Neil Postman sent a note declaring it was the best paper McLuhan had written from a left-brain point of view. I had written up our paper that first night after our luncheon discussion as though I was writing a physics paper, hence the left-brain bias.

References

Carpenter, Edmund, and Marshall McLuhan. *Explorations: Studies in Culture and Communication* 1, iii, 1953.

Forsdale, Louis. "Marshall McLuhan and the Rules of the Game." *The Antigonish Review* 74–5 (1988): 172–81.

Kuhn, Thomas S. *The Structure of Scientific Revolutions* (1st ed.). Chicago: University of Chicago Press (2nd ed. 1970; 3rd ed. 1996), 1962.

Lamberti, Elena. *Marshall McLuhan's Mosaic: Probing the Literary Origins of Media Studies.* Toronto: University of Toronto, 2012.

Logan, Robert K. *McLuhan Misunderstood: Setting the Record Straight.* Toronto: The Key Publishing House, 2013.

Logan, Robert K., and Marshall McLuhan. *The Future of the Library: From Electric Media to Digital Media.* New York: Peter Lang Publishing, 2016.

Marchand, Philip. *Marshall McLuhan: The Medium and the Messenger.* Toronto: Random House, 1989.

McLuhan, Eric. "Marshall McLuhan's Theory of Communication: The Yegg." *Global Media Journal* 1, no. 1 (2008): 25–43.

McLuhan, Marshall. *The Gutenberg Galaxy: The Making of Typographic Man.* Toronto: University of Toronto Press, 1962.

McLuhan, Marshall. *Understanding Media: Extensions of Man.* New York: McGraw Hill, 1964. (The page references in the text are for the McGraw Hill paperback second edition. Readers should be aware that the pagination in other editions is different.)

McLuhan, Marshall. "Casting my Perils before Swains." In *McLuhan Hot and Cool*, edited by Gerard Emanuel Stearn. New York: Dial Press, 1967a.

McLuhan, Marshall. "The New Education." *The Basilian Teacher* 11, no. 2 (1967b): 66–73.

McLuhan, Marshall. "Playboy Magazine Interview." *Playboy* 16, no. 3 (March, 1969): 53–74, 158.

McLuhan, Marshall. "Education in the Electronic Age." *Interchange* 1 no. 4 (1970): 1–12.

McLuhan, Marshall. "Marshall McLuhan Convocation Address, The University of Alberta", 1971. http://projects.chass.utoronto.ca/mcluhan-studies/v1_iss5/1_5art3.htm. Accessed April 16, 2019.

McLuhan, Marshall. "The Future of the Book." In *Understanding Me: Lectures & Interviews*, edited by Stephanie McLuhan and David Staines. Toronto: McClelland & Stewart, 1972.

McLuhan, Marshall. "Communication: McLuhan's Laws of Media." *Technology and Culture* 16, no. 1 (1975): 74–78.

McLuhan, Marshall. "Laws of Media." *English Journal* 67, no. 8 (1977): 92–94. Also published *Et Cetera* 34, no. 2: 173–79.

McLuhan, Marshall. "II. Media Evolution, Media Forms, Language and Speech." In *Essential McLuhan*, edited by Eric McLuhan and Frank Zingrone. Concord Ontario: Anansi, 1995.

McLuhan, Marshall. "The Medium is the Massage." In *Understanding Me: Lectures and Interviews*, edited by Stephanie McLuhan and David Staines. Cambridge, MA: MIT Press, 2005a.

McLuhan, Marshall. *Marshall McLuhan Unbound*, Vol. 19, edited by W. Terrence Gordon. Corte Madera, CA: Gingko Press, 2005b.

McLuhan, Marshall, and Quentin Fiore. *The Medium is the Massage: An Inventory of Effects*. New York: Random House, 1967.

McLuhan, Marshall, and George B. Leonard. "The Future of Education: The Class of 1989." *Look Magazine*, Feb 21 (1967): 23–25.

McLuhan, Marshall, and Wilfred Watson. *From Cliché to Archetype*. New York: The Viking Press, 1970.

McLuhan, Marshall, and Robert K. Logan. "Alphabet, Mother of Invention." *Et Cetera* 34, no. 4 (1977): 373–83.

McLuhan, Marshall, and Robert K. Logan. "The Double Bind of Communication and the World Problematique." *Human Futures* (Summer 1979): 1–3.

McLuhan, Marshall, and Eric McLuhan. *Laws of Media: The New Science*. Toronto: University of Toronto Press, 1988.

McLuhan, Marshall, and David Carson. *The Book of Probes*. Corte Madera, CA: Gingko Press, 2003.

Molinaro, Matie, Corrine McLuhan, and William Toye (eds). *Letters of Marshall McLuhan*. Toronto: Oxford University Press, 1987.

Needham, Joseph. *The Grand Titration*. Toronto: University of Toronto Press, 1956.

Nevitt, Barrington, and Maurice McLuhan. *Who Was Marshall McLuhan?* Toronto: Stoddart Publishing, 1994.

Wolfe, Tom. "The New Life Out There." *The New York Herald Tribune*, 1965. http://archive.wphna.org/wp-content/uploads/2015/03/1965-NYHT-Tom-Wolfe-on-Marshall-McLuhan.pdf. Accessed May 21, 2021.

CHAPTER TWO

The Ten Elements of McLuhan's General Theory of Media

In this chapter I will describe the ten elements that I believe comprise McLuhan's General Theory of Media indicating how they are intertwined. They include his use of or notions of the following:

(1) probes;
(2) figure/ground: the key element in McLuhan's general theory of media;
(3) the medium is the message;
(4) the subliminal nature of ground or environment revealed only by the creation of an anti-environment;
(5) the reversal of cause and effect among other reversals;
(6) the importance of percept over concept, the human sensorium and media as extensions of man;
(7) the division of communication into the oral, written, and electric ages and the notions of acoustic and visual space;
(8) the notion of the global village;
(9) media as environments and media ecology; and
(10) the Laws of Media.

(1) McLuhan's Probes

In undertaking to identify McLuhan's methodology it is important to keep in mind that he often made use of probes as a form of exploration. One of the aspects of McLuhan's writing style that makes it so challenging and controversial is his constant use of these probes. A probe for McLuhan was a hypothesis that he would explore not because he thought it was correct, but because he found it interesting and believed that it might lead to new insights. Unlike most academics, McLuhan was more interested in making new discoveries than in always being correct. Scott Taylor (Marchand 1989, 149) who interviewed McLuhan in 1960 wrote, "McLuhan thought he just had to get as many ideas out as possible, to utter or 'outer' them, and let the environment decide which were important and which were not." Even his mistakes provide insights. Because McLuhan was constantly probing, constantly trying out new ideas, not everything he said panned out as planned. The way in which McLuhan used the term probe is described in *The Book of Probes* (McLuhan and Carson 2003, 403): "The probe is a means or method of perceiving. It comes from the world of conversation and dialogue as much as from poetics and literary criticism. Like conversation, the verbal probe is discontinuous, nonlinear; it tackles things from many angles at once."

It was with this in mind that he uttered what seemed to be the self-contradictory remark, "I don't necessarily agree with everything I say." What he was basically saying was that in exploring one of his probes, he was attempting to see where an idea would carry him rather than trying to prove something he believed to be true. A scientist who formulates a hypothesis does not necessarily believe that it is true. In fact, as Karl Popper (1959) once declared, for a proposition to be considered scientific it must be falsifiable. McLuhan embraced this tenet of the scientific method. He functioned as a scientist. He observed the effects of media and then hypothesized and considered his hypotheses as probes that might or might not be true. McLuhan even suggested a third option. A hypothesis might be half-true, which McLuhan declared would be a lot of truth. He did not need to be exactly correct every time; he only had to keep exploring. He was also fond of pointing out the close connection between the words probe and prove. In fact, one cannot prove anything by using the methods of science because if one were to prove that a proposition was true then it could not be falsified; and hence by Popper's criteria that for a proposition to be scientific it must be falsifiable, the proposition proven to be true would not be a scientific proposition (Logan 2003). One can only probe and test.

(2) Figure/Ground: The Key Element in McLuhan's General Theory of Media

Of all of McLuhan's various techniques and methods I believe that his use of the figure/ground relationship derived from gestalt psychology holds the key to understanding his General Theory of Media and in fact is the ground or basis for his GToM. In Gestalt psychology the behavior of an individual must be understood in the context of the whole pattern or gestalt of their psyche. I believe another possible influence in McLuhan's formulation of his figure/ground analysis in addition to gestalt psychology was his former PhD supervisor at Cambridge University, I. A. Richards, who developed the notion of feedforward. I. A. Richards, who coined the expression, held that for a speaker or writer to have their message properly understood, the speaker or writer had to feedforward the context of what they were saying. In other words, the background or context of an assertion is essential for fully understanding that assertion. The notion of feedforward together with that of feedback became the backbone of cybernetics and the general systems approach. Feedforward was also incorporated by McLuhan in terms of his figure/ground analysis and it served as the ground of McLuhan's treatment of media and their impacts.

Another influence on McLuhan was Ludwig von Bertalanffy, the founder of general systems theory whose work McLuhan read. Figure/ground analysis is based on the idea that one cannot understand an object of study in isolation from the system or environment in which it operates. For McLuhan a figure and the environment or ground in which it operates forms a system in which the system as a whole, in turn, influences the way the figure behaves and the figure changes the nature of the system. McLuhan used the terms ground and environment interchangeably but never wrote explicitly of or used the term systems theory even though his approach was certainly a systems approach. We will return to the influence of Bertalanffy in Chapter Five where we discuss McLuhan's use of general systems theory in his understanding of media and his development of media ecology.

A third possible influence was Freud. McLuhan wrote, "While Poe and the Symbolists were exploring the irrational in literature, Freud had begun to explore the resonant figure/ground double-plot of the conscious and unconscious (McLuhan, M. and McLuhan, E. 1988, 52)."

The figure is the usual object under study, whether it is a tool, a technology, a medium of communication or even the content of a medium of communication. The figure is that of which we are directly aware, and it is for the most part the focus of our attention. The ground is the environment in which the figure operates and its effects are subliminal. It is also the case that the ground or environment is also created in part by that figure whether it is a tool, a technology, or a medium of communication. "Any new technology, and extension or amplification of human faculties when given material embodiment, tends to create a new environment (McLuhan 2005b, Vol. 4, 6)." "Figures rise out of, and recede back into, ground (McLuhan, M. and McLuhan, E. 1988, 5)."

One can only fully understand the figure in the context of the ground or environment in which it operates and which it helps to create. The same figure operating in different grounds or contexts have different meanings and different effects. Every medium, every technology creates its own unique environment or ground which is subliminal, that is, not obvious to its users. The interaction of a medium or technology with the environment or ground it creates is one of both feedforward and feedback. The figure feedforwards to the environment and the environment feeds back to the figure. The technology or medium gives rise to an environment which changes that technology or medium, which changes the environment in an infinite loop of feedforwards and feedbacks. The interactions between the two, the technology or medium and its environment are dynamic.

When McLuhan says "figures rise out of, and recede back into, ground (ibid.)," he is suggesting that there is a dynamic relationship between figure and ground which is lost on most observers because of the subliminal nature of ground. According to McLuhan in a letter to Tom Stepp dated March 26, 1973,

> The figure is what appears and the ground is always subliminal. Changes occur in the ground before they occur in the figure. We can project both figure and ground as images of the future using the ground as subplot of subliminal patterns and pressures and effects which actually come before the more or less final figures to which we normally direct our interest (Molinaro, McLuhan, C. & Toye 1987, 194).

McLuhan's technique of figure/ground entails a pairing of two elements: the figure of which we are immediately aware and the ground which is subliminal. It is the ground that McLuhan focuses on before invariably working back to the figure. This, I believe, is the basis of or ground in McLuhan's General Theory of Media. I will support this hypothesis by induction by considering a number of examples from many of McLuhan's key analyzes and observations each of which involve him beginning with ground and then working back to the figure. Let's begin with a quote from his essay, "The End of the Work Ethic" in which he points out that with electric media there is a flip or reversal from figure to ground: "The present fact is that we all live in this new resonating simultaneous world in which the relation between figure and ground, public and performer, goal-seek and role-playing, centralism and decentralism have simply flipped and reversed again and again (McLuhan 2005a, 194)."

I suggested above that McLuhan's figure/ground analysis might have evolved from gestalt psychology or the idea of I. A. Richards notion of feedforward. But McLuhan claimed that it is electric media that create a "new resonating simultaneous world" making use of figure and ground and their reversal absolutely necessary.

Our awareness of figure and ground are quite different. The figure is what we are consciously aware of, which we first perceive and receives most if not all of our attention. It is the first thing we notice. The ground or the environment is something that we are not immediately aware of and its effects are for the most part subliminal. The figure is the technology or medium we are using or trying to understand. The ground is the environment that the medium or technology creates through its use and, paradoxically, in which it also operates. The medium actually creates the ground in which it operates. McLuhan observed that "environments are not just containers but are processes that change the content totally (McLuhan 1995, 275)."

According to McLuhan most users of a medium or a technology are only aware of the figure of the medium or the technology itself. They are for the most part oblivious to the ground or environment which the tool creates and in which it operates. The one exception to this is the artists and scientists that McLuhan defines as people "of integral awareness" (McLuhan 1964, 71). He defines the artist in very broad terms. "The artist is the man in any field, scientific or humanistic, who grasps the implications of his actions and of new knowledge in his own time. He is the man of integral awareness (McLuhan 1964, 65)." It is the artists as defined by McLuhan who create an anti-environment, another key element of McLuhan's GToM that reveals the environment created by a medium or technology and its effects. But it can also be a scientist operating as an artist. "Scientists make their discoveries as 'artists,' not specialists. Such scientists construct experiments as 'works of art' to probe the environment (McLuhan, M. & E. McLuhan 2011, 55)." Based on this definition of McLuhan's, I believe, we may regard McLuhan as both an artist and a scientist.

When we receive information content through some medium of communication our focus is almost exclusively on the information being conveyed to us and we are almost largely or completely ignorant of the effects of the medium that carries that message. When we make use of some technology the same dynamics applies. Many think of what we can do with that technology or what that technology allows us to do and give very little or no thought to what the use of that technology does to us other than achieving the function to which we apply it. For example, we think of the automobile strictly in terms of how it gets us from point A to point B quickly, comfortably and conveniently. We do not consider how the automobile has changed the dynamics of city life where we give priority to the movement of cars over that of pedestrians. The consequence of this is that urban life does not have the convivial ambience that cities once had before the advent of the automobile when people walked to work and shopping and knew their neighbors as they passed them in the streets.

What McLuhan introduced with his focus on ground rather than figure was a much deeper understanding of what media and technology do to us other than merely achieving the functions or tasks we put them to. Because the environment that media/technology create is subliminal many believe that technology is neutral. To use a phrase that McLuhan loved to employ "the problem with those that believe technology is neutral is that 'their fallacy is all wrong.'"

I believe that the notion of technological neutrality dates back to the very first tool makers and users. Their focus was strictly on the immediate task or function they could achieve with their tool. They were too busy surviving to think about whether the tools had other impacts other than the use they put them to. So, the idea that technology is neutral has been with us since time immemorial, an idea that was finally put to rest by Marshall McLuhan.

McLuhan's Use of Figure/Ground Analysis Led to Many Other Insights

Let us now consider a number of examples of McLuhan's use of the figure/ground dichotomy which he often formulated in terms of one-liners and show how each of these involved his reversal first from ground in which the figure operates to the figure itself.

The Arts, Literature and Language

"The audience, as ground, shapes and controls the work of art (McLuhan, M. and McLuhan, E. 1988, 48)." In this example he begins with the audience, the ground to consider how it effects the figure of the work of art. McLuhan suggested that the figure/ground relationship was key in understanding the medium of language as his following two quotes demonstrate: "Language always preserves a play or figure/ground relation between experience and perception and its replay in expression (ibid., 121)." "All words at every level of prose and poetry and all devices of language and speech derive their meaning from figure/ground relations (McLuhan and Carson 2003, 236–37)."

Jokes and Grievances

McLuhan (https://www.azquotes.com/quote/1369551, accessed April 19, 2019) observed that, "when people become too intense, too serious, they will have trouble in relating to any sort of social game or norm. Perhaps this is why jokes are so important. On one hand, they tell us about where the problems and grievances are, and, at the same time, they provide the means of enduring these grievances by laughing at the problems." In terms of figure/ground, the joke is the figure and the grievance, which prompts the joke, is the ground.

Service and Disservice of Technology

"All I am saying is that any product or innovation creates both service and disservice environments which reshape human attitudes (Molinaro, McLuhan, C., and Toye 1987, 404)." It is the service of technology that one is aware of and hence is the figure whereas the disservice of technology that is subliminal is ground. Here is another McLuhan reversal in that a new technology is developed because of the service it provides but unbeknownst to its users it also reverses into some forms of disservice which are subliminal. The disservices of the new technology emerge in the subliminal ground that the new technology creates.

The Content of a New Medium is an Older Medium

"Except for light, all other media come in pairs, with one acting as the content of the other, obscuring the operation of both (McLuhan 1995, 274)."

> The content of any medium [A] is always another medium [B]. The content of writing is speech, just as the written word is the content of print, and print is the content of the telegraph. If it is asked, 'What is the content of speech?' it is necessary to say, 'It is an actual process of thought, which is itself nonverbal (McLuhan 1964, 6 {[A] and [B] are my insertions})

It is the other medium [B] that is the content of the medium [A]. Medium [B] is the figure and medium [A] is the ground. In the content of writing is speech, it is writing which is the figure and speech that is the ground.

There is another dimension to the relationship of a new medium and an older medium when it comes to the transition into the mechanical technologies that followed in the wake of the printing press and the transition from the mechanical technologies to electric technologies in that the older medium not only become the content of the new medium but also it becomes the ground of the new medium as McLuhan suggested in the Introduction to the 2nd Edition of Understanding

Media: "The medium is the message means, in terms of the electronic age, that a totally new environment has been created. The 'content' of this new environment is the old mechanized environment of the industrial age ... We are aware only of the 'content' of the old environment (McLuhan 1964, vi)."

Interdisciplinarity versus Specialization

McLuhan made use of figure and ground in understanding interdisciplinarity versus specialization in the age of electric information. "Centuries of specialist stress in pedagogy and in the arrangement of data now end with the instantaneous retrieval of information made possible by electricity ... The specialist is one who never makes small mistakes while moving towards the grand fallacy (McLuhan 1964. 383 & 136)." McLuhan's interdisciplinary approach allowed him to identify the large patterns of the interplay between a society and its technologies. "In education the conventional division of the curriculum into subjects is already as outdated as the medieval trivium and quadrivium after the Renaissance. Any subject taken in depth at once relates to other subjects (McLuhan 1964, 301)." In the consideration of specialization versus interdisciplinarity it is the interdisciplinary approach that focuses on ground while it is the specialist approach that focuses on figure.

Task Force and Crowd Sourcing versus Specialization

McLuhan saw that with electrically configured information that crowd sourcing and task forces would replace the monopolies of knowledge and the individual expert of the literate age. He wrote (McLuhan 1971):

> There is no kind of problem that baffles one or a dozen experts that cannot be solved at once by a million minds that are given a chance simultaneously to tackle a problem. The satisfaction of individual prestige, which we formerly derived from the possession of expertise, must now yield to the much greater satisfactions of dialogue and group discovery. The task yields to the task force.

In the consideration of monopolies of knowledge versus crowd sourcing or the task force it is crowd sourcing or the task force that is focused on ground and the monopolies of knowledge that are focused on figure.

Pattern Recognition versus a Point of View

Consideration of pattern recognition versus a point of view involves a focus on ground rather than figure. "The effects of technology do not occur at the level of opinions or concepts but alter sense ratios or patterns of perception steadily and without any resistance (McLuhan 1964, 18)." "We are now living in a world where things change so rapidly that anybody can spot the configuration, the pattern of change and we're living increasingly in a world of pattern recognition (http://www.marshallmcluhanspeaks.com/electric-age/1967-pattern-recognition/ accessed April 23, 2019)." "Faced with information overload, we have no alternative but pattern-recognition (McLuhan 1969b)." In contrasting the point of view approach with that of pattern recognition it is pattern recognition that is oriented to ground and the concept or point of view approach that is oriented to figure.

Figure and Ground in Education

McLuhan used his distinction between figure and ground to advocate for a change in education with a focus on questions and discovery rather one on answers and instruction. "We are entering the new age of education that is programmed for discovery rather than instruction (McLuhan 1964, x)."

> Ivan Illich has a book called *Deschooling Society* in which he argues that, since we now live in a world where the information and the answers are all outside the schoolroom, let us close the schools. Why spend the child's time inside the school giving him answers that already exist outside? It's a good question, but his suggestion to close the schools is somewhat unnecessary. Instead of putting the answers inside the school, why not put the questions inside (McLuhan 1970b).

McLuhan is suggesting that more could be learned from discussing all possible answers to questions than memorizing the canonical answers to these questions. In his consideration of procedures in schools, McLuhan sees that answers or packaged information play the role of figure and the questions for exploration that of ground and is once again advocating for a reversal from consideration of figures to a consideration of ground.

Subjective versus Objective

For McLuhan's consideration of subjective and objective thought patterns it is the subjective thought patterns that are ground and the objective thought patterns that are figure.

Waves versus Particles

Even in the world of physics he thought in terms of figure/ground. He saw the focus of Newtonian mechanics was on figure whereas the focus of quantum mechanics was on ground. He embraced Bohr's complementarity principle in quantum mechanics where particles behaved like waves and waves behave like particles. Light is both a wave and a particle and the electron is both a particle and a wave. In the modern physics of field theory, which influenced McLuhan's thinking, the field or wave associated with a particle is the ground and the particle, whether it is an electron or a photon, itself is the figure.

Sputnik versus the Planet Earth

Perhaps the most outrageous figure/ground pairing was the one McLuhan made of Sputnik and the planet Earth. "Sputnik ... maybe an extension of the planet itself .... Nature ended ... the planet became an art form, an ecologically programmable environment (McLuhan 2005a, 208)." Sputnik is the figure and the planet is the ground.

A Cool Medium versus a Hot Medium

One of McLuhan's interesting distinctions of media was his notion of hot and cool media.

> There is a basic principle that distinguishes a hot medium like radio from a cool one like the telephone, or a hot medium like the movie from a cool one like TV. A hot medium is one that extends one single sense in "high definition," the state of being well filled with data ... a cool medium or one of low definition ... because so little is given ... so much has to be filled in by the listener ... Hot media are, therefore, low in participation, and cool media are high in participation or completion by the audience. Naturally, therefore, a hot medium like radio has very different effects on the user from a cool medium like the telephone (McLuhan 1964, 24).

A hot medium is one that is high definition that does not require the user to fill in any missing parts and as such it is more figure-like than ground-like. A cool medium is one of low definition that requires the audience to fill in the gaps and as a consequence is more ground-like.

There is an element of a reversal in hot and cool media in the sense that with the transition from the mechanical media that followed in the wake of the printing press to that of electric media there was a transition by and large from hot media to cool media.

I would like to close this discussion of figure/ground with two probes, which is a way of saying I am about to speculate. As McLuhan observed, what was unique about his approach to understanding media was his use of figure/ground analysis and his focus or emphasis on the ground rather than the figure, on effects rather than causes, on disservice rather than service, on the anti-environment rather than environment, on the medium rather than the message, and on the user rather than the content. His focus on each of these dyadic pairs was in many ways the exact opposite to that of other media scholars. And by his own admission he used hyperbole to get his point across because he was running against the usual flow in communications studies.

The second probe is my belief that it took a highly literate thinker to have come up with the figure/ground approach that McLuhan developed. The notion of figure/ground with which McLuhan analyzes media including electric ones arises from a literary perspective in which figure and ground can be distinguished. With the acoustic space of oral communication and electric-configured communication there is no figure and ground; there is only a field. McLuhan is operating out of the literary tradition quite to the contrary of the claim of some that he is a captive of electric communication. In fact, McLuhan, in my opinion, was attempting to preserve the literary tradition and trying to rescue us from the insidious invasion of television culture. Happily, because of the ubiquity of computing with personal computers, smart phones and the Internet the obsolescence of written text by television has been reversed because text has become a much greater percentage of the content of digital media compared to the mass electric media that dominated communications in McLuhan's day. Many of the patterns of electric communications that he identified such as decentralization, interdisciplinarity, the shrinking of the gap between producers and consumers, the exchange of jobs for roles and knowledge becoming the driver of our economy have persisted with digital media and have in fact grown more pronounced as we shall see in section (7) Communication in the Oral, Written, and Electric Ages; Acoustic and Visual Space.

Conclusion of McLuhan's Figure/Ground Analysis

We have examined a number of examples of how McLuhan's technique of distinguishing figure and ground and his figure/ground analysis has led to a variety of insights. As we now turn to describe the other basic elements of McLuhan's GToM we will see that many of them also entail a consideration or derive from McLuhan's figure/ground methodology, that is, the pairing of the two elements of (1) the figure of which we are immediately aware and (2) the ground which is subliminal. It is the ground that McLuhan focuses on before invariably working back to the figure. I believe that the figure/ground analysis is the basis of McLuhan's General Theory of Media. I remind the reader of McLuhan's claim that "the relation between figure and ground …[has] simply flipped and reversed again and again (McLuhan 2005a, 194)." In the next section we examine McLuhan's most famous figure/ground analysis, namely the one-liner, "the medium is the message," in which the content of a medium is the figure and the medium itself is the ground.

(3) "The Medium is the Message"

McLuhan's focus on ground rather than figure is a key element in his understanding of media and represents what makes his approach so unique. His famous one-liner "the medium is the message" incorporates this reversal of attention from figure to ground. The content is the figure and the medium is the ground or environment. "The medium is the message" is McLuhan's way of saying to understand the effects of media one needs to focus on the effects of the medium independent of its content. What is important in McLuhan's GToM is not only identifying the figure and its ground but also the interaction between them. "In all patterns, when the ground changes, the figure too is altered by the new interface (McLuhan 2005a, 180)." In other words, the same figure in two different environments behave differently. A person in their work place is different than a person socializing with friends or engaging in their favorite hobby.

The concern with the figure/ground relationship is consistent with McLuhan's emphasis on interface and pattern rather than on a fixed point of view. It also explains why he thought that content was not independent of the medium in which it was transmitted. The medium forms a ground for the content that it transmits and as such changes the message and this is another reason that McLuhan claimed the medium is the message. The message of a medium independent of its content is the ground that it creates for any content it transmits. So, a medium actually possesses two messages, one is a figure or its content and the other is its ground, the ground it creates for its content and the way its changes or colors that content.

Marshall McLuhan (1964, 5) introduced his signature one-liner to the world, "the medium is the message," on page 5 of the opening Introduction to his 1964 book *Understanding Media: Extensions of Man*:

> THE MEDIUM IS THE MESSAGE
>
> In a culture like ours, long accustomed to splitting and dividing all things as a means of control, it is sometimes a bit of a shock to be reminded that, in operational and practical fact, the **medium is the message.** This is merely to say that the personal and social consequences of any medium-- that is, of any extension of ourselves -- result from the new scale that is introduced into our affairs by each extension of ourselves, or by any new technology (bolding is mine).

The term "the medium is the message," which I have bolded then appears 7 more times in *Understanding Media* in the following passages:

> "**the medium is the message**" because it is the medium that shapes and controls the scale and form of human association and action. The content or uses of such media are as diverse as they are ineffectual in shaping the form of human association. Indeed, it is only too typical that the "content" of any medium blinds us to the character of the medium (ibid., 6).

> Specialized segments of attention have shifted to total field, and we can now say, "The medium is the message" quite naturally. Before the electric speed and total field, it was not obvious that **the medium is the message**. The message, it seemed, was the "content," as people used to ask what a painting was about (ibid., 19).

> If people are inclined to doubt whether the wheel or typography or the plane could change our habits of sense perception, their doubts end with electric lighting. In this domain, **the medium is the message**, and when the light is on there is a world of sense that disappears when the light is off.

> As the missile is a self-contained transportation system that consumes not only its fuel but its engine, so light is a self-contained communication system in which **the medium is the message** (ibid., 140).

> In any given structure, the rate of staff accumulation is not related to the work done but to the intercommunication among the staff, itself. [In other words, **the medium is the message**] (ibid., 290).

> Although **the medium is the message**, the controls go beyond programming. The restraints are always … directed to the "content," which is always another medium. So, the effects of radio are quite independent of its programming. To those who have never studied media, this fact is quite … baffling (ibid., 337).

> Vehemence of projection of a single isolated attitude they mistake for moral vigilance. Once these censors became aware that in all cases "**the medium is the message**" or the basic source of effects, they would turn to suppression of media as such, instead of seeking "content" control (ibid., 350).

McLuhan's Alternative Expression for The Medium is the Message

In letters to Edward T. Hall and Buckminster Fuller, McLuhan formulated an alternative expression for the medium is the message: "To say that any technology or extension of man creates a new environment is a much better way of saying the medium is the message (in a letter to Edward T. Hall dated September 16, 1964 in Molinaro, McLuhan, C. & Toye)." In a 1964 letter to Bucky Fuller, Marshall expressed a similar notion: "If one says that any new technology creates a new environment that is better than saying the medium is the message (ibid., 308–09)."

The Medium is the Message and Figure/Ground Reversal

McLuhan's one-liner of "the medium is the message" often confuses the reader because of the irony that McLuhan deployed in its formulation. Let us first consider a medium of communication like the book or TV. There is the content of the medium, the text in the case of a book and the show in the case of TV. The text is obviously the message of the book and the show the message of TV. But these contents are not the messages that McLuhan is referencing in his one-liner, "the medium is the message." Let us refer to the explicit content of the medium as their primary message. Because McLuhan posited that a medium like a book or a TV have an effect independent of their content it is these effects independent of their content that McLuhan identifies as the message, an implicit message actually, in his one-liner "the medium is the message." Let us call this implicit message the secondary message. McLuhan chose to formulate his idea of the existence of this secondary implicit message of a medium by saying "the medium is the message." Because the content of a communication medium is a message, which we have labeled as the "primary message" is so obvious, McLuhan deigns not to mention it perhaps because of his fondness for irony or his desire to shock. Translating McLuhan's "medium is the message" using our definition of the "secondary message," McLuhan's one-liner, becomes "the medium is the 'secondary message'." In other words, there are two messages to a medium, the primary message which is the explicit content of the medium and the implicit message or secondary message which is the effect of the medium independent of its explicit or primary content. The primary message is figure and the secondary message is ground.

Clarifying the role of figure and ground in our understanding of "the medium is the message," it is the medium that is the ground and the "secondary message" and it is the content or the "primary message" that is the figure. The reversal in McLuhan's "the medium is the message" is that most people focus of the figure of the content of the medium, the "primary message" whereas he focuses on the medium and its effects independent of its content, the "secondary message."

When the medium is a technology like the motor car and not a communications medium the relationship between figure and ground is more complicated and there are two ways of interpreting "the medium is the message" and the figure/ground relationship. In scenario number 1, we can regard the car as a medium and its passengers as its content. In this case the car is the medium and the passengers are its content. In scenario number 2, we can regard the car as a figure operating in the ground of the services needed to support its operation. It is no longer a medium as was the case in scenario number 1. This is the sense of what I said earlier when I wrote the medium creates the ground in which it operates. The car did not literally create the services needed for its operation but it was the existence of the car that motivate the web of services necessary for its successful operation. McLuhan described this scenario number 2 when he was interviewed by Maclean's Magazine in Toronto.

> When I say that the medium is the message, I'm saying that the motor car is not a medium. The medium is the highway, the factories, and the oil companies. That is the medium. In other words, the medium of the car is the effects of the car. When you pull the effects away, the meaning of the car is gone. The car as an engineering object has nothing to do with these effects. The car is a figure in a ground of services. It's when you change the ground that you change the car. The car does not operate as the medium, but rather as one of the major effects of the medium. So "the medium is the message" is not a simple remark …. It really means a hidden environment of services created by an innovation, and the hidden environment of services is the thing that changes people. It is the environment that changes people, not the technology (McLuhan 1980).

What McLuhan is essentially saying here is that any new technology creates a new environment. The message of any medium is not just the content that it carries or the tasks that it enables, but rather the sum total of all the changes that it produces in the world, thereby transforming it. The message of cars, for example, is all of the infrastructure created to support them as McLuhan just suggested in the above quote; the auto industry, highways, the petroleum industry, gas stations, etc.; it is also the resulting pollution, gridlock and deaths from autos and one can even add the suburbs, an environment that surround the inner city that only the automobile made possible – in other words, the message of the car is the totality of the changes wrought by cars.

The convenience that the figure of the motor car provides is obvious. What is not obvious is the subliminal effects of the ground or environment that the automobile creates or generates. One example is the pollution and gridlock just mentioned. Another that was alluded to earlier is the way the city has been restructured to facilitate the movement of automobiles rather than creating an environment with vibrant neighborhoods. Another example is that the automobile has created the suburbs adding hours to the work day because of the time to commute back and forth from a home in the suburbs to work in the city's downtown. Another dehumanizing factor of suburban life is that people drive to a shopping mall instead of walking to a neighborhood store and as a consequence do not get to know their neighbors other than the folks that live on either side of their house. They even drive to a health club to get exercise, which seems counter intuitive.

One misunderstood point of this famous one-liner made by some is the notion that "the medium is the message" only applies to media of communication. In fact, McLuhan regarded media as not only communications tools but technology in general. For him a medium was anything that mediated one's interaction with their environment or surroundings and with other individuals. Accordingly, all tools, which he considered as extensions of our body, are media. "The media can be viewed as artificial extensions of our sensory existence (McLuhan 1955)." Speech, writing, the printing press and the computer were all lumped together with the hand axe, the hammer, the automobile and the space ship and included both hardware and software. He believed, "since all media are extensions of ourselves, or translations of some part of us into various materials, any study of one medium helps us to understand all others (McLuhan 1964, 139)." This being the case McLuhan analyzed both communication media and other tools under the single category of media. And given that all tools form an ecosystem they have to be studied using media ecology (see Section 9. Media as Environment and Media Ecology below) as content analysis would not incorporate all of the interactions of media with each other.

Another misinterpretation of "the medium is the message" is that some have taken it literally claiming the content is the message. McLuhan clarified this in his famous Playboy interview where he said, "I'm not suggesting that content plays no role – merely that it plays a distinctly subordinate role (McLuhan 1969a)."

Another Meaning of "The Medium is the Message"

"The Medium is the Message" has more than one meaning. The one that we have discussed so far is the notion that a medium has its own intrinsic effects on our perceptions independent of its content in the case of communication media or the functions it performs in the case of tools. This is the medium's unique message independent of its content or its function. But there is still another meaning to "the medium is the message," which is that a medium transforms its content, which is particularly true for communication media. The same content delivered in two different media will not have the same effect on those receiving that content. This is an idea that McLuhan elucidated on a number of occasions during our Monday night seminars at his Coach House on the campus of St. Michael's College at the University of Toronto.

I have not found an explicit mention of this idea in McLuhan's oeuvre so I will have to reference it as private communication (If any reader knows of a reference please contact me at logan@physics.utoronto.ca). I did find, however, the following passage which provides a vague reference to this idea. In the essay "The Relation of Environment to Anti-Environment" McLuhan (2005b Vol. 4, 7) writes, "The effects of TV on the movie go unnoticed, and the effects of the TV environment in altering the entire character of human sensibility and sensory ratios is completely ignored." The first clause gets at the notion that a medium transforms its content so that the same content in different media have different effects on its users. A movie on television has different effects from the same movie viewed in a cinema. The second clause incorporates the idea that a medium has effects independent of its content.

A movie shown on television will not have the same effect as one seen in a movie theater. A play that is made into a movie will not have the same effects as a play performed with live actors in a theater even if the script is identical for the two productions. In fact, actors that perform for a live audience and for a movie camera report that they are totally different performance experiences. Reading a novel and then seeing a play or a movie based on the novel are two totally different experiences.

Even a telephone conversation on a cell/smart phone is different than one on a landline. There is a certain intimacy with a landline or a house telephone that a conversation on a cell phone lacks. There is also another major difference which is that many more people become addicted to a smart phone than to a cell phone or a land-line telephone. My result of googling "telephone addiction" resulted in finding hundreds of articles about cell or smart phone addiction but none on landline addiction. I then tried googling landline telephone addiction with almost the identical result but this time I found an article entitled "I got a Landline to Fix My iPhone Addiction-Vice (www.vice.com/en_us/article/j53k93/i-got-a-lanline-to-save-my-brain, accessed May 9, 2019)." The smart phone addiction is obviously due to all the features in addition to voice communication such as being a terminal to email and the Internet, being a camera and a place to store photos, audio files and video files.

Commercial cinemas in recent years no longer project movies on their screen using light shining through a roll of semi – transparent film. Instead they make use of the medium of digital video. Commercial movies are now all in the video format. The film format has been discontinued except for the production of some non-commercial art films. Many older movies made with film have been converted to the video format for showings in commercial cinemas or on TV. The same movie shown in the video and the film formats are markedly different. What is lacking with the videoed movies is what was called "the magic of the silver screen." Atom Egoyan, a Canadian film maker and four-time winner at the Cannes Film

Festival, explained to me that with video the filmmaker can no longer get a true black on the screen, that is, the total absence of light. He explained that as a movie maker there were effects, he could not do with video that he could do with film and that he considered movies made with film and those made with video as two different media.

(4) The Subliminal Nature of the Ground of a Medium That Is Revealed by the Creation of an Anti-Environment

The notion of an anti-environment is a fundamental element of McLuhan's GToM. It is a tricky concept so let me identify its relationship to a medium and the subliminal environment or ground that the medium creates. In this section we will be considering a medium, A; the subliminal ground or environment, B, that it creates and in which it operates; and the antienvironment, C, which allows us to become aware of that subliminal environment, B, of the medium, A. The relationship of a medium A, its subliminal environment B and the anti-environment C that allows us to become aware of B is complex which is why I have labeled these elements as A (the medium), B (the subliminal environment of A) and C (the anti-environment that allows us to become aware of the subliminal environment B). Hopefully the labeling of A, B and C will help the reader follow the complex relationships among A, B and C used throughout Section (4).

The Subliminal Effects of Technology

"Man remains as unaware of the psychic and social effects of his new technology as a fish of the water it swims in (McLuhan 1969a)." One of the central themes of McLuhan's approach to understanding media and technology is his claim that we are unaware of the subliminal effects of media. "All technological extensions of ourselves must be numb and subliminal, else we could not endure the leverage exerted upon us by such extension (McLuhan 1964, 264)."

"Media effects are new environments as imperceptible as water to a fish, subliminal for the most part (McLuhan 1969b, 22)." Despite our being unaware of the subliminal effects of a medium such as A, they act as "living vortices of power creating hidden environments that act abrasively and destructively on older forms of culture (McLuhan 1972, v)."

The Complex Figure/Ground Relationships of the Medium A, Its Environment or Ground B and the Anti-Environment C that Reveals the Subliminal Nature of B

In terms of McLuhan's figure/ground division applied to the relationship of the medium A and the subliminal environment, B that A creates, A is figure and B is ground.

But in terms of McLuhan's figure/ground division applied to the relationship of the anti-environment, C, that reveals the subliminal environment, B, and the subliminal environment, B itself, it is the case that B is the figure and C is the environment in which B operates. This is the tricky part. B is the ground for the figure A but then in its relationship with C, B becomes the figure and in the ground of C. In other words, it switches roles from being the ground of A to being the figure in the ground of C. Recapping: A is the figure in the ground of B and the B becomes the figure in the ground of C. A is to B as B is to C.

The Anti-Environment

It takes a special kind of thinker to consider the impact of the use of a tool other than the immediate function it allows one to achieve. The effects of a technology other than the task to which it is put is contained in the environment or ground that the use of the technology or medium creates and those effects are subliminal. The subliminal environment of a technology or medium is only revealed by the creation of an anti-environment by a person "of integral awareness" such as an artist or a scientist as McLuhan has suggested.

It is the anti-environment, C, created by the artist or scientist that allows us to become aware of the ground or environment, B, which the medium, A, creates and in which A operates. It is only when the artist or the scientist creates an anti-environment, C, that we are able to see the environment, B, and hence the subliminal effects of the medium or technology, A.

McLuhan's Description of The Complex Figure/Ground Relationships of a Medium, Its Environment and the Anti-Environment

Having explained this complex relationship of a medium, A, its subliminal environment, B, and the anti-environment, C, created by an artist or a scientist here is how McLuhan describe these relationships in his own words.

"New environments are always invisible. It is the preceding environment that is always blamed for the damage done by the new one ... The Greek word for environment is perivallo, which means to strike from all side at once (McLuhan 1968)."

"Environments are invisible. Their groundrules, pervasive structure, and overall patterns elude easy perception (McLuhan & Fiore 1967, 68)."

Any new technology, any extension or amplification of human faculties given material embodiment, tends to create a new environment ... It is in the interplay between the old and new environments that there is generated an innumerable series of problems and confusions ... It is useful to view all the arts and sciences as acting in the role of anti-environments that enable us to perceive the environment (McLuhan 1967a).

Technologies tend to be unconscious as much in their origin as in their effects. A new technology enjoys a brief reign as an anti-environment. Then in it becomes environment in turn. The need for the anti-environmental seems to be deeply grounded, as with dream and sleep (Molinaro, McLuhan, C. & Toye 1987, 315).

The role of the artist [and scientist] is to create an Anti-environment as a means of perception and adjustment. Without an Anti-environment, all environments are invisible. (McLuhan and Carson 2003: 30–33).

To summarize, it is the artist or the scientists by creating an anti-environment that allows us to perceive the new environment that is created by a new medium or technology. If it was not for this anti-environment, we would only see the content or function of the new medium and not the environment that supports the new medium but which at the same time is generated by that new medium. In other words, a new medium creates the environment or ground in which it operates. A new medium gives rise to an environment whose effects and impacts are subliminal to most users of that medium. The artist or scientist creates an anti-environment that reveals the environment of the new medium under consideration and hence the subliminal effects of the new medium. The anti-environment operates as the ground to the figure of the environment which in turn is the ground to the figure of the new medium under consideration. Let A be the medium and B its environment. B is the ground of the figure A. Let C be the anti-environment that reveals B. Then C is the ground for the figure of B. My apologies to the reader for the repetitiveness, but the relationship of a medium, the environment it creates and operates within and the anti-environment that allows us to recognize the subliminal environment is extremely complex.

Given the abstract nature of McLuhan's notion of the anti-environment let us turn to some concrete examples. One of the reversals we just reviewed was the figure ground relationship of the joke and the grievance where the joke is the figure and the grievance is the ground. McLuhan and Fiore (1967, 92) analyze humor in terms of his notion of anti-environment: "Humor as a system of communications and as a probe of our environment—of what's really going on—affords us our most appealing anti-environmental tool. It does not deal in theory, but in immediate experience, and is often the best guide to changing perceptions."

Comedians are artists who creates an anti-environment that reveals the grievances of their audience through their jokes and stories. The same is true of the writer of certain novelists that reveal the hidden ground of the social interactions of their society. The novels of humorist Mark Twain Huckleberry Finn and Tom Sawyer acted as an anti-environment revealing the racist ground of American life through the figures of his protagonists Huckleberry and Tom.

It is not just humorists that create anti-environments through their writing. One of the greatest creations of an anti-environment is the story of Rachel Carson's authorship of Silent Spring in 1962 which launched the environmental movement and revealed the subliminal effects of the medium of DDT and other pesticides. McLuhan suggested that the best candidates for creating an anti-environment was an artist or a scientist. As it turns out Rachel Carson was both as she was trained as a marine biologist and worked in that capacity for the U.S. Bureau of Fisheries and she was a gifted science writer. According to Science History Institute. "Carson's power did not stem from a charismatic personality but lay in her scientific knowledge and poetic writing (https://www.sciencehistory.org/historical-profile/rachel-carson, accessed May 31, 2020)." The anti-environment that Rachel Carson created was her award winning book Silent Spring. It revealed the subliminal ground of the medium of pesticide chemicals especially DDT. The medium of pesticides especially DDT where an effective technology in increasing the productivity of commercial agriculture and eliminating some very annoying pests such as fire ants. The subliminal ground of the pesticides that the advocates of the widespread use of these toxic chemicals were not aware of was the collateral damage to the physical environment. The compelling story that Rachel Carson told in her book *Silent Spring* "marked the turning point in society's understanding of the interconnections between the environment, the economy, and social well-being (ibid.)."

(5) The Reversal of Cause and Effect and Other Reversals

Beginning with Effects and Working Round to Causes

At the beginning of this study I mentioned that I planned show that McLuhan's reversals of figure and ground; concepts and percepts; cause and effect; visual and acoustic spaces; a medium and its content and the fourth Law of Media are interconnected together with his systemic ecological field approach and they form the basis of his GToM. In this section we will focus on a number of reversals beginning with the reversal of cause and effects, one of the more central reversals in McLuhan's GToM.

McLuhan reversed the order of cause and effect by focusing on the effects and then examining the causes that gave rise to those effects. There is a clear connection with his figure/ground analysis as causes such as a medium are figures and their effects are ground and subliminal so that the reversal of cause and effect parallels the reversal of figure and ground. He wrote,

> My writings baffle most people simply because I begin with ground and they begin with figure. I begin with *effects* and work round to the *causes*, whereas the conventional pattern is to start with a somewhat arbitrary selection of 'causes' and then try to match these with some of the effects. It is this haphazard matching process that leads to fragmentary superficiality. As for myself, I do not have a point of view, but simply work with the total situation as obvious *figures* against hidden *ground* (Molinaro, McLuhan, C, and Toye 1987, 478).

McLuhan's justification or motivation for reversing the focus on cause and effect is contained in the following quote: "The way to study the effects, for example, if you wanted to study what the motor car was, you might find out more from what it did to the environment and the community (McLuhan 2005a, 90)." Studying the effects of a technology has a practical aspect to it in that it identifies the problems that the technology creates because every technology provides as McLuhan once suggested provides both service and disservice (Molinaro, McLuhan, C., and Toye 1987, 404).

McLuhan also suggested that the best way to study media was by "making inventories of effects (ibid.)." I would therefore suggest that the best way to continue and carry on the work of McLuhan is to make an inventory of all the technologies that have emerged since his passing in 1980, which happens to mark the beginning of the era of personal computers, the Net, the Web, smartphones and what we popularly refer to as the digital age. Technically mainframe computers made use of digital technology but because they were only accessible to a narrow range of technical experts I would mark the emergence of the personal computer, the PC, as the break boundary between the electric age of mass media and the digital age of today.

The Artist's, Scientist's and Inventor's Reversal of Cause and Effect

McLuhan's consideration of the reversal of cause and effect was influenced by the work of artists, inventors and scientists. The method of the scientists is to observe effects and by experimentation and reasoning to determine the causes of the observed effects. McLuhan also saw the creative process of both the inventors and the artists as working backwards from the effects they wanted to create to the causes that would lead to their desired effects.

> A. N. Whitehead ... explained how the great discovery of the nineteenth century was the discovery of the technique of discovery. Namely, the technique of starting with the thing to be discovered and working back, step by step, as on an assembly line, to the point at which it is necessary to start in order to reach the desired object. In the arts this meant starting with the effect and then inventing a poem, painting, or building that would have just that effect and no other (McLuhan 1964, 68).

As a scholar of literature and the arts McLuhan observed that artists begin with the effect they are trying to create and then find the elements that will create that effect they wish to achieve. McLuhan incorporated this technique in his scholarship as he related in the above quote. This is one example of how McLuhan operated as both a scientist and an artist at the same time making use of the arts and science to derive some of his insights. He is unique in this respect combining insights from both the arts and the sciences, something we noticed earlier when I listed the thinkers who influenced him which included both those from the sciences and the arts. The consideration of McLuhan as an artist also helps explains the aphoristic poetic style in which he expressed his insights unlike almost all of his colleagues in academia. McLuhan's study of literature and his association with writers/poets like Wyndham Lewis and Ezra Pound had a great influence on his writing style.

There is also another dimension to McLuhan's somewhat cryptic writing style which is that he

> enjoyed being a trickster. Jokes and joking were part and parcel of his persona and his research methodology. Helga Haberfellner, a former McLuhan student, reported that she once heard McLuhan say that puns were the crossroads of meaning, a form of parataxis. No wonder so many straight-laced academics found him and his techniques incomprehensible. McLuhan took jokes quite seriously because of the insights they provide. He once wrote, "I am indebted to funnyman Steve Allen for the observation that all jokes are based on grievances. I ran that backward and got, where there are grievances there are jokes." The hidden grievances behind McLuhan's jokes was that he saw with great clarity the effects of electric media but most of his colleagues were unable to see that. His other grievance was that his critics were unable to see the value of his probes, which gave rise to his crack, "Do you think my fallacy is all wrong? (Logan 2011, 27)

An example of reversal of cause and effect that I remember McLuhan citing was his remark that the effect of the telegraph was the cause of the telephone, which I discovered he first made in a letter to Ashley Montagu: "more and more I feel compelled to consider causation as following effects. The effects of the telegraph created an environment of information that made the telephone a perfectly natural development (Molinaro, C., McLuhan, and Toye 1987, 446)." There is a similar relationship of the elevator and the skyscraper. Elisha Otis's *"first safety elevator for passengers was for a building just five **storeys** high, the E.V. Haughwout & Co. store in New York. But his invention would make the skyscraper possible, transforming skylines around the world* (Toronto *Globe & Mail* of March 2017)." The effect of the safety elevator was the cause of the skyscraper.

The Reversal in the Laws of Media

McLuhan's figure ground analysis and the reversal of cause and effect led to a number of other reversals that characterized his GToM. We already encounter a major use of the reversal in the fourth law of the Laws of Media: "And when pushed far enough, the new medium, technology or human-made artifact reverses or flips into a complementary or possibly an opposite form (McLuhan 1975)." We might also think of the third law which states that a new medium retrieves something from the past as a reversal of something that had been obsolesced.

McLuhan's Use of Reversals in *Understanding Media* and Their Connection to Electrically Configured Information

Although the Laws of Media and the fourth law in particular was not formulated until the mid 1970s in the two papers McLuhan (1975, 1977) published introducing the LoM he actually made use of this idea of reversals in 1964 in his seminal work *Understanding Media: Extensions of Man* (McLuhan 1964). In fact, the entire Chapter three entitled "Reversal of the Overheated Medium" deals with reversals. The term reverse or reversal appears 55 times in *Understanding Media*. Here are two excerpts from that book that illustrate McLuhan's focus on reversals. They are presented in the order in which they appear in the book:

> After three thousand years of specialist explosion and of increasing specialism and alienation in the technological extensions of our bodies, our world has become compressional by dramatic reversal. As electrically contracted, the globe is no more than a village. Electric speed in bringing all social and political functions together in a sudden implosion has heightened human awareness of responsibility to an intense degree. (McLuhan 1964, 4)

> So, the greatest of all reversals occurred with electricity, that ended sequence by making things instant. With instant speed the causes of things began to emerge to awareness

again, as they had not done with things in sequence and in concatenation accordingly. Instead of asking which came first, the chicken or the egg, it suddenly seemed that a chicken was an egg's idea for getting more eggs (ibid., 10).

These last two quotes from *Understanding Media* reveal where McLuhan might have been stimulated to think about reversals as he saw that electrically configured information created a reversal from the patterns of the linear sequential visual forms of organization characteristic of the literate age to the all at once acoustic forms of organization that characterized oral society. This is purely speculative on my part but when he says, "the greatest of all reversals occurred with electricity," it is apparent that he was thinking in terms of reversals and attributed this reversal to electric information traveling at the speed of light. For example, here are two quotes describing the reversals brought about by electricity: "the hardware world tends to move into software form at the speed of light (McLuhan 2005a, 276)" and "the electronic age … angelizes man, disembodies him. Turns him into software (McLuhan 1996b)." He also wrote, "the electronic age is a world in which causes and effects become almost interchangeable, as in music structures (https://citas.in/frases/1733143-marshall-mcluhan-the-electronic-age-is-a-world-in-which-causes-and/, accessed July 14, 2019)."

The Reversal of the Overheated Medium

In Chapter Three The Reversal of the Overheated Medium in *Understanding Media* (McLuhan 1964, 45–51): McLuhan wrote:

> The principle that during the stages of their development all things appear under forms opposite to those that they finally present is an ancient doctrine. Interest in the power of things to reverse themselves by evolution is evident in a great diversity of observations, sage and jocular (ibid., 46).

> The stepping-up of speed from the mechanical to the instant electric form reverses explosion into implosion. In our present electric age, the imploding or contracting energies of our world now clash with the old expansionist and traditional patterns of organization (ibid., 47).

The Reversals as West goes East and East goes West

Another reversal McLuhan identified related to the electrification of information and the emergence of the global village was that cultures were moving towards a universal global culture.

Associated with this transformation of the real world into science fiction is the reversal now proceeding apace, by which the Western world is going Eastern, even as the East goes Western. Joyce encoded this reciprocal reverse in his cryptic phrase: "The West shall shake the East awake While ye have the night for morn" (ibid., 46–47).

The Reversals of the City and the Countryside

McLuhan also saw that as the world turned into a global village not only were Eastern and Western cultures becoming more uniform but a similar process of homogenization of the city and the country side was also taking place as they began to reverse their traditional roles.

> Today the road beyond its break boundary turns cities into highways, and the highway proper takes on a continuous urban character. Another characteristic reversal after passing a road break boundary is that the country ceases to be the center of all work, and the city ceases to be the center of leisure. In fact, improved roads and transport have reversed the ancient pattern and made cities the centers of work and the country the place of leisure and of recreation (ibid., 44).

The User is the Content

"The audience, as ground, shapes and controls the work of art (McLuhan, M. and McLuhan, E. 1988, 48)." In McLuhan's consideration of the public and the performer it is the public or audience that is the ground and the performer that is the figure. In the consideration of the reader and the author it is the reader that is the ground and the author that is the figure. These last three comparisons lead to McLuhan's famous one liner: "the user is the content" in which he is claiming that it is the interpretation of the user that is the content because the user is the ground. The content of the technology or medium that the user is interpreting is the figure. In this example McLuhan is once again reversing cause and effect so that the cause is the figure and the effect, that is, the interpretation, is the ground. "The user is the content of any situation, whether its driving a car, or wearing clothes or watching a show (McLuhan 1976)."

The Reversal of Jobs and Roles

Over 40 years ago McLuhan detected a shift in the way in which some members of the professional workforce were pursuing their careers. Rather than remaining with the same company throughout their career a number of professionals did not see a life-long job as their ultimate goal but rather they began to see how their training and their work experiences prepared them to take on different assignments where they could gain new skills and advance their effectiveness. They saw each assignment they took on as a way to advance themselves and make a greater contribution to their society. They were not looking for the security of a life-long job but rather they were seeking to play a role in society, which at the same time benefitted both them and their society. Because of his willingness to reverse the order in which conventional scholars analyzed their society McLuhan was able to see that "in the electronic age … you cannot have jobs; you can only have a role (McLuhan 2005a, 155)." In the 40 or so years since McLuhan developed that insights it is now the norm for workers to pursue a role rather than focus on a job particularly a life-long job. The mobility of workers from one company is even greater today in the digital age than it was over 40 years ago when McLuhan first made this observation and hence is another example of his making accurate predictions. In McLuhan's consideration of the relationship of jobs and roles it is the role that is the ground and the job that is the figure. "Goal seeking" is figure and "role-playing" is ground.

The Rearview Mirror View of the World

Another example of McLuhan's use of reversals was his notion of the rearview mirror view of the world in which he suggests that we drive into the future using only our rearview mirror. "The past went that-a-way. When faced with a totally new situation, we tend to attach ourselves to the objects, to the flavor of the most recent past. We look at the present through a rear-view mirror. We march backwards into the future (McLuhan and Fiore 1967, 75–76)."

> Most people … still cling to what I call the rearview-mirror view of their world. By this I mean to say that because of the invisibility of any environment during the period of its innovation, man is only consciously aware of the environment that has preceded it; in other words, an environment becomes fully visible only when it has been superseded by a new environment; thus, we are always one step behind in our view of the world. Because we are benumbed by any new technology — which in turn creates a totally new environment — we tend to make the old environment more visible; we do so by turning it into an art form and by attaching ourselves to the objects and atmosphere that characterized it (McLuhan 1969a).

More McLuhan Reversals

"The photograph reverses the purpose of travel, which until now had been to encounter the strange and unfamiliar (McLuhan 1995, 287)."

> "As technology advances, it reverses the characteristics of every situation again and again. The age of automation is going to be the age of do it yourself (ibid., 283)."

"Every process pushed far enough tends to reverse or flip suddenly. Chiasmus — the reversal to process caused by increasing its speed, scope or size (McLuhan & Nevitt 1972, 6)."

Another indication of McLuhan's fascination with reversals was that he often would mention Thorstein Veblen's saying that "invention is the mother of necessity" in his lectures or his Monday night seminars. Veblen's remark also illustrates the reversal of cause and effect.

In the next section, Section 6 we will encounter more reversals namely the reversal from concepts to percepts and the reversal from media as extensions of man to amputations due to media. In Section 7 we will encounter reversals associated with the transition from oral to written to electric communication, the reversal associated with acoustic and visual space, and the reversal of left and right hemispheric thought patterns. Reversals associated with the emergence of electric communication include the reversal of mechanical forms, the reversal of specialism, the reversal of centralization. In Section 8 we will encounter the reversal into the global village. For a complete list of all the McLuhan reversals see Chapter Six.

(6) The Importance of Percept over Concept, the Human Sensorium and McLuhan's Notion of "Media as Extensions of Man"

"The percept takes priority of the concept (Letter to Edward T. Hall, 1971 in Molinaro, McLuhan, C., and Toye 1987, 397)."

> "Effects are perceived, whereas causes are conceived. Effects always precede causes in the actual developmental order (McLuhan & Carson 2003, 303)."

Percepts versus Concepts

Just as McLuhan made a distinction between figure and ground as well as cause and effect and reversed the emphasis of these pairs beginning with the latter and then finally getting around to the former, he made a similar reversal with concepts and percepts. He always began with percepts and then moved to an associated concept. For McLuhan percepts are ground and concepts are the figure and it is with the ground that the true effects of a medium are felt and not with the figure of the medium's content or the medium itself.

> Our conventional response to all media, namely that it is how they are used that counts, is the numb stance of the technological idiot. For the 'content' of a medium is

like the juicy piece of meat carried by the burglar to distract the watchdog of the mind. The effects of technology do not occur at the level of opinions or concepts, but alter sense ratios or patterns of perception steadily and without any resistance. The serious artist is the only person able to encounter technology with impunity, just because he is an expert aware of the changes in sense perception (McLuhan 1964, 18).

Inspired by the artist's ability to perceive change due to the effects of new media and new technologies McLuhan (1969a) concluded the following:

> Because inherent in the artist's creative inspiration is the process of subliminally sniffing out environmental change. It's always been the artist who perceives the alterations in man caused by a new medium, who recognizes that the future is the present, and uses his work to prepare the ground for it. But most people, from truck drivers to the literary Brahmins, are still blissfully ignorant of what the media do to them; unaware that because of their pervasive effects on man, it is the medium itself that is the message, not the content, and unaware that the medium is also the message—that, all puns aside, it literally works over and saturates and molds and transforms every sense ratio. The content or message of any particular medium has about as much importance as the stenciling on the casing of an atomic bomb. But the ability to perceive media-induced extensions of man, once the province of the artist, is now being expanded as the new environment of electric information makes possible a new degree of perception and critical awareness by nonartists (McLuhan 1969a).

McLuhan was also fond of quoting Wyndham Lewis, who wrote: "The artist is always engaged in writing a detailed history of the future because he is the only person aware of the nature of the present." McLuhan believed that the artist's insights were like radar or an early warning system, which could pick up the social and cultural problems and challenges that new technologies created.

McLuhan's focus on observation also contributed to his focus on percepts rather than concepts. The field approach used in the physical sciences for the non-linear dynamics of complex systems in which causal relations flow in both directions contributed to his method of reversing cause and effect where he started with the effects and worked backwards to their causes. This aspect of his methodology was equally influenced by his observations of the methods of artists who he observed to also work backwards from the effects they wanted to create to the materials or causes of their art form.

The Notion of the Sensorium and the Effects of Media on the Senses

McLuhan believed that the effects of a medium or technology was its effect on the sensorium, that is, how it affected our senses. "A theory of cultural change is impossible without knowledge of the changing sense ratios effected by various externalizations of our sense (McLuhan 1962, 49)." He also wrote, "the use of any kind of medium or extension of man alters the patterns of interdependence among people, as it alters the ratios among our senses (McLuhan 1964, 91)."

> All media work us over completely. They are so persuasive in their personal, political, economic, aesthetic, psychological, moral, ethical, and social consequences that they leave no part of us untouched, unaffected, unaltered. The medium is the massage. Any understanding of social and cultural change is impossible without a knowledge of the way media work as environments. All media are extensions of some human faculty – psychic or physical. ... Media, by altering the environment, evoke in us unique ratios of sense perception. When these ratios change, men change ... Environments are not passive wrappings, but active processes, which work us over completely, massaging the ratio of the senses and imposing their silent assumptions. But environments are invisible. Their ground-rules, pervasive structure, and overall patterns elude easy perception (McLuhan and Fiore 1967, 26, 41 & 68).

When McLuhan says above, "media work as environments" he is formulating for the first time the notion of media ecology. He is also applying Bertalanffy's (1968) notion of General Systems Theory to media studies. We will explore this idea in greater detail in Chapter Five.

Media as Extensions of Man

Another key element of McLuhan's GToM is the notion that media are extensions of their users as evidenced by the title of his 1964 book *Understanding Media: Extensions of Man.*

"The wheel is an extension of the foot, the book is an extension of the eye, clothing, an extension of the skin, electric circuitry, an extension of the central nervous system (McLuhan and Fiore 1967, 31–40)."

> All technologies are extensions of our physical and nervous systems to increase power and speed. Again, unless there were such increases of power and speed, new extensions of ourselves would not occur or would be discarded. For an increase of power or speed in any kind of grouping of any components whatever is itself a disruption that causes a change of organization (McLuhan 1964, 99).

Because media become extensions of ourselves, we become enamored of them and in a certain sense there is a reversal in which we are no longer in control of them, but they begin to control us because we are unaware of their subliminal effects. McLuhan described this phenomenon in terms of Greek myth of Narcissus (the Greek word for narcosis), who fell in love with his image in a pond of water and as a result became paralyzed by it and fell into a narcotic state of numbness and became a closed system, "a servomechanism of his own extended or repeated image (McLuhan 1964, 47)."

> A special property of all social extensions of the body is that they return to plague the inventors in a kind of *agenbite of outwit*. As Narcissus fell in love with an outering (projection, extension) of himself, man seems invariably to fall in love with the newest gadget or gimmick that is merely an extension of his own body. Driving a car or watching television, we tend to forget that what we have is simply a part of ourselves stuck *out there*. Thus disposed, we become servo-mechanisms of our contrivances, responding to them in the immediate, mechanical way that they demand of us.
>
> The point of the Narcissus myth is not that people are prone to fall in love with their own images, but that people fall in love with extensions of themselves which they are convinced are not extensions of themselves. This provides, I think, a fairly good image of all of our technologies, and it directs us towards a basic issue, the idolatry of technology as involving a psychic numbness (McLuhan 1996a).
>
> To behold, use or perceive any extension of ourselves in technological forms is necessarily to embrace it. By continuously embracing technologies, we relate ourselves to them as servo-mechanisms (McLuhan 1964, 52).

At first, technology serves as an extension of humankind but after a while a subliminal flip or reversal takes place and suddenly the user is transformed into an extension of the technology they have come to consider part of them. This idea has been expressed in the following oft-quoted remark: "We become what we behold. We shape our tools and thereafter our tools shape us." This quote has been attributed to McLuhan who used it a lot in his seminars and in his every day conversations, but it was actually coined by John Culkin (1967).

As we become servo-mechanisms of our technologies, our media, which are extensions of us. reverse into auto-amputations.

> The principle of self-amputation as an immediate relief of strain on the central nervous system applies very readily to the origin of the media of communication from speech to computer … Any invention or technology is an extension or self-amputation of our physical bodies, and such extension also demands new ratios or new equilibriums among the other organs and extensions of the body (McLuhan 1964, 52 & 54).

Although the following reversal, which I formulated, was not one made by McLuhan it is one inspired by him. McLuhan's media as extensions of man reverses into man as extensions of his media in the digital age with today's social media. "With digital media … there is a flip or reversal in which man or the user of digital media becomes an extension of those digital media as these media scoop up our data and use them to the advantage of those that control these media (Logan

2018)." The data of the user becomes an extension of the digital media they use so one can say that man becomes an extension of his digital media, the exact reverse of McLuhan's notion of media as an extension of man. We will explore this idea in greater detail in Chapter Four.

(7) Communication in the Oral, Written, and Electric Ages: The Nature of Acoustic and Visual Space

McLuhan treated all forms of technology whether they involved communication or not as media. However, communication media in terms of the spoken word, written communication and electrically configured information played a particularly important role in McLuhan's analysis of media and technology. A journal he co-edited with Edmund Carpenter from 1953 to 1972 was called *Explorations: Studies in Culture and Communication* indicating the importance of communication media.

Issues # 1 to # 8 of *Explorations* have been reprinted and published by Wipf and Stock (Carpenter and McLuhan 2016). Issue #9 was published in 1959 as the book *Eskimo* by Carpenter (1959). Issues #10 to #32 which ran from 1960 to 1972 as inserts in the University of Toronto alumni magazines are now available online. Links to these 23 issues can be found in an article entitled Links to Explorations Issues #10 to #32 plus Tables of Contents of all Explorations Issues #1 to #32 that was published in the open access online journal *New Explorations: Studies in Culture and Communication*. It is a revival of the original journal Exploration whose editor just happens to be your author. It is available online at https://jps.library.utoronto.ca/index.php/nexj/index (accessed July 2, 2020). I hope the readers will forgive me for this plug for the journal *New Explorations*.

"The medium is the message" gave rise to two of McLuhan's closely related key insights, namely the division of human history into the three communications ages of oral, written and electric communication as well as the related division between acoustic space and visual space. Oral and electric communication basically operate in acoustic space and written communication operates in visual space. These three forms of communication, oral, written and electric, more so than any other media (i.e. other forms of non-communicative technology), created environments which impacted all forms of technology and how they were used. These three classes of communication media also impacted the way that societies organized their forms of governance, work, education, and social interactions more so than any of the other forms of technology. Some non-communicative technologies had more of an impact on society than others, the automobile versus the bicycle for example.

The division of human history into the 3 communication eras of oral, written and electric communication provided a framework for McLuhan's GToM.

The era of the oral tradition begins with the emergence of Homo sapiens and human speech and was superseded once a society achieved literacy. The age of literacy begins in Summer 5000 years ago and stretches to the discovery of electricity and its use in the form of the telegraph in the middle of the 19th Century. McLuhan divides the age of writing is further subdivided into three periods. The first period of writing begins with the invention of written symbols in the form of ideographic writing such as Sumerian ideographs, Egyptian hieroglyphics and Chinese characters (still in use today). The second period of written communication begins with the invention of the phonetic alphabet in the middle of the 2nd millennium among the Kennites or copper miners of the Sinai desert (McLuhan and Logan 1977; Logan 2004a), and the third period of writing begins with the invention of the typographic Gutenberg printing press (McLuhan 1962). The third communication era, that of the electric flow of information, covers the period from the first use of the telegraph in 1844 to the present.

A number of media ecologist (Levinson 1999; Logan 2016; Strate 2017) make a distinction between the electric age and the digital one, which is a distinction McLuhan never made as he never experienced the digital media of personal computers, the Internet, the World Wide Web and the smartphone. Sadly, the stroke that incapacitated him in 1979 occurred just as the first primitive personal computers were beginning to appear. I believe that if McLuhan would have lived into the digital age he would have differentiated the electric age of mass media from the digital age as I did in my paper The Five Ages of Communication (Logan 2002). The dissemination of electronic digital information parallels in some ways that of electric information but there is a very important difference. The users of electric media on the whole are merely passive consumers of information whereas the users of digital media can interact actively with the information they access and most importantly with each other. The electric age was basically an age of broadcast whereas the digital age is an age in interactivity in which every user is a creator of content through their emails, tweets, blogs, vlogs, podcasts, videocast, YouTube or Vimeo channels or their use of social media.

During each of these major communication eras, socio-economic and cultural life were deeply affected by the dominant medium of communication. As each new mode of communication had an impact on society, it dominated those which had preceded it, not obsolescing them, but dramatically changing their character and the use to which they were put. Speech or the oral tradition naturally survived both literacy and electricity but its function changed. It retained its dominance for face-to-face conversation and everyday communication; however, it was no longer used as the repository of a culture's traditions as it had been in Homer's time nor the means of spreading news from one village or country to another. With writing, the spoken word took on new functions, sometimes becoming an art form in the guise of poetry and theater. Each new medium used the previous media as its content as McLuhan (1964, 267) observed, "the 'content'... is always another medium. The content of the press is literary statement, as the content of the book is speech, and the content of the movie is the novel."

Just as the spoken word underwent change in its form and uses so too was writing transformed with the advent of electricity. With the telegraph the written word became more terse and tighter. The telegraph also changed the newspaper as news reports could be wired from across the globe. Electricity and the instantaneous flow of information changed the psychic environment of authors, causing them, in McLuhan's words, to "*live mythically and in depth*" (McLuhan 1964, vii). As a consequence, writers became concerned with psychology, anthropology, and sociology. The psychological novel and stream-of-consciousness technique were born. With writing, education was transformed from the apprenticeship mode of learning on the job to formal schooling for children and the rise of institutions of higher learning and research such as occurred in ancient Babylon, Egypt, and Greece. The printing press gave rise to the modern school system of mass education. It also became the model for the assembly-line style of mass production. The mass media of radio, telecommunications and television shrunk the world to the dimensions of a global village as did the Internet to an even greater degree.

Centralization versus Decentralization in the Three Ages of Communication

In the age of oral communication before there was writing the structures of society were decentralized. Without the written word there was no way for a centralization of power to emerge. With writing, however, command and control at a distance by a centralized political entity was possible, at first in the form of a city state, then a nation state and eventually by an empire. Not long after writing made its first appearance in different parts of the world empires began to emerge, first in Mesopotamia, then in Persia, Greece, Rome, India, China, Meso-America and Peru. Centralization with writing not only impacted political structures but also commerce and industry. With electricity, however, centralization began to give way to decentralized structures as observed by McLuhan (1964, 47 & 65):

> Electricity does not centralize but decentralizes. It is like the difference between a railway system and an electric grid system: the one requires rail-heads and big urban centers. Electric power, equally available in the farmhouse and the Executive Suite,

permits any place to be a center, and does not require large aggregations ... The implosion of electric energy in our century cannot be met by explosion or expansion, but it can be met by decentralism and the flexibility of multiple small centers.

McLuhan further developed this theme when he suggested that, "In the age of circuitry, of feedback, fragmentation and specialism tend to yield to integral forms of organization ... Circuitry is a profoundly decentralizing process."

Societies Imitate Their Technologies

McLuhan observed that the fragmentation and centralization of industrial or mechanical society was reversed in the electric age of information to systems of integration and decentralization which retrieved many of the aspects of the social organization of preliterate society. These observations were based on the following set of assumptions:

- The dominant tools or technologies of a society create patterns of usage which infiltrate or penetrate the social structures of a society.
- These patterns of usage change those structures.
- Eventually, the social structures come to imitate or replay the patterns by which these dominant technologies are organized.

Visual versus Acoustic Space

The observation of the differentiation of the oral tradition and the age of literacy was not unique to McLuhan but was a well-established theme by many scholars who pre-dated McLuhan's publication in 1962 of the Gutenberg Galaxy where he first introduced the notion of acoustic and visual space. The earliest scholars to describe the oral tradition were Vuk Stefanovic Karadzic (1972) and Sir James Frazer (1890) both active in the 19th century, and Millman Parry (2019) active in the early 20th century. McLuhan was also influenced by a number of his contemporaries who also wrote about the oral tradition including Albert Lord (1960), Eric Havelock (1963), Harold Innis (1951, 1972), Mircea Eliade (1958), Walter Ong (1958) his former student and Edmund Carpenter (1959) with whom he co-edited the journal *Explorations*.

McLuhan developed the notion of acoustic space to describe the oral tradition given that the primary flow of information was through the spoken word and hence that information passed through the ear and was therefore acoustic. Because that acoustic based information could come at one simultaneously and from all directions, McLuhan therefore defined acoustic space as having its center everywhere and its margins nowhere. Acoustic space was one of the key ideas introduced in Marshall McLuhan's understanding of media and an integral part of his GToM. McLuhan contrasted acoustic space with the visual space that characterized literate communication with writing especially alphabetic writing and print because of the way the written word is accessed by the eye as opposed to the ear. "The interiorization of the technology of the phonetic alphabet translates man from the magical world of the ear to the neutral visual world (McLuhan 1962, 21)." In visual space information that passes exclusively through the eye is linear and is processed sequentially, one thing at a time.

The contrast between visual and acoustic space became one of McLuhan's defining characteristics of media ecology. His definition of acoustic space, as center everywhere and margins nowhere, comes from the way by which auditory signals are received where ever one finds oneself (and hence center everywhere) and from all directions at the same time (and hence no margins). Acoustic space as oral information comes at us from all direction at once and surrounds us.

In acoustic space, not only sound but also data and information come at you from all directions at once. It is simultaneous and instantaneous. Visual space, on the other hand, is sequential and linear. "The visual sense, alone of our senses, creates the forms of space and time that are uniform, continuous and connected (McLuhan 2005b, Vol. 4, 15)."

McLuhan claims that before the alphabet was invented and before there was wide-spread print media, the world was acoustic. Oral poetry was the popular culture of the time. Nothing was set in stone, and so information and stories would change depending on the context in which they were experienced. The epics of Homer belong in the acoustic tradition. When writing was developed, the world was plunged into a visual world. History was written on a linear, 2-dimensional plane. Information was regarded as true if it stood the test of time. But it was subject to being destroyed. Information was not privy to change. With the advent of electric information, such as the telephone, radio and television, McLuhan claimed that society was entering a new acoustic age. McLuhan understood the transition from oral to written to electric communication in terms of the transition from acoustic space to visual space and back again to acoustic space.

McLuhan had extended the notion of "acoustic space" to also. describe the conveyance of electric-based information via telegraph, telephone, radio, television, and would certainly have added digital media that he so presciently foresaw, if he had lived on into the digital age. His assignment of acoustic space to electric information was based on the fact that like orally transmitted information, the electric-based information comes from all directions at once. The difference is that oral information arrives locally but electric information arrives from all over the globe. Although he did not live to see the emergence of the digital age and world of hypertext he somehow foretold of its arrival.

McLuhan was one of the first, perhaps the very first, to describe and emphasize the differences between the ages of written and electric communication and the radical difference between the two. Another unique McLuhan contribution was that he pointed out that the written tradition could be further subdivided into three sub-ages, associated respectively with ideographic writing, the use of the phonetic alphabet and, finally, typographic print. According to McLuhan the written word was visual, linear and sequential and this characteristic of writing became even more pronounced with the transition from ideographic writing to alphabetic writing and was again stepped up with the emergence of the Gutenberg printing press.

There was also a figure/ground dimension to McLuhan's division to the three eras of communication. He suggests that ground rather than figure predominates in both oral and electric cultures but in the era of the written word and especially with mechanical culture that emerged with the printing press figure comes to the fore and ground recedes into the subliminal. He also suggested that the structures of written culture are centralized whereas as those of both oral and electric culture are decentralized. This is consistent with his figure/ground analysis as centralized structures are figure-like whereas decentralized structures are ground-like.

I believe that McLuhan's notion of acoustic space which he defined as the center is everywhere and margins nowhere is actually rooted in his background as a medieval scholar and perhaps because he was a practicing Roman Catholic. As pointed out by Findlay-White and Logan (2016), McLuhan's definition of acoustic space as "center everywhere and margin nowhere" is almost identical to a 12th Century definition of God found in *The Book of the 24 Philosophers* (in Latin *Liber XXIV philosophorum*), which lists 24 "sentences," "aphorisms" or "definitions" of "God": "God is the intellectually knowable sphere whose center is everywhere and whose circumference is nowhere." This definition was used by many theologians and philosophers. The list includes Alain de Lille, Meister Eckhart, Nicholas of Cusa, Giordano Bruno, Robert Fludd, Blaise Pascal, Gottfried Wilhelm Leibniz and Jorge Luiz Borges. I do not believe that the parallel in the definition of God and acoustic space is a mere coincidence as McLuhan as a devout Catholic would have been familiar with much of this literature. It is also consistent with his notion that God is a percept and not a concept.

The Origin of McLuhan's Notion of Acoustic Space

McLuhan's application of the notion of acoustic space can be traced as far back as 1957 to his collaboration among his circle of colleagues at the University of Toronto (The Toronto School), and those who participated in the journal *Explorations* that McLuhan and Ted Carpenter co-edited. McLuhan developed this notion based on a suggestion from his colleague, Carl Williams, a psychology professor at the University of Toronto and a former student of E. A. Bott. Edmund Carpenter documented this trade off in his memorial documented by Theall (2001, 241):

> Carl provided the first breakthrough. He used the phrase 'auditory space' in describing an experiment by E. A. Bott ... the phrase was electrifying. Marshall changed it to 'acoustic space' and quoted symbolist poetry. Jackie [Tyrwhitt] mentioned the Indian city of Fatehpur Sikri. Tom [Easterbrook] saw parallels in medieval Europe. I talked about Eskimos.

McLuhan, on the other hand, made acoustic space an integral part of his emerging GToM. He saw it as the perfect way to describe the oral tradition and the characteristics of electrically configured information.

> Acoustic Space has the basic character of a sphere whose focus or center is simultaneously everywhere and whose margin is nowhere ... Acoustic space is dynamic; it has no fixed boundaries. It is space created by the method or process itself. In contrast, visual space is static and container-like, with a fixed center and margin (McLuhan and Powers 1989, 74).

Acoustic Space in the Electric Age

We begin with McLuhan's description of the electric age. "The electric age gave us the means of instant, total field-awareness ... We live today in the Age of Information and of Communication because electric media instantly and constantly create a total field of interacting events in which all men participate ... (McLuhan 1964, 47, 203)." "Electric media, because of their total 'field' character, tend to eliminate the fragmented specialties of form and function that we have long accepted as the heritage of alphabet, printing, and mechanization (ibid., 228)." "In the West, electronic technology displaces visual space and retrieves acoustic space in a new form, as the ground now includes the detritus of alphabetic civilization (McLuhan M. and E. McLuhan 1988, 106)."

> In the electric age, when our central nervous system is technologically extended to involve us in the whole of mankind and to incorporate the whole of mankind in us, we necessarily participate, in depth, in the consequences of our every action. It is no

longer possible to adopt the aloof and dissociated role of the literate Westerner … The electric implosion now brings oral and tribal ear-culture to the literate West (ibid., 5 & 46).

According to McLuhan (1964, 233) all of the effects of the Gutenberg press reverse with electric media as we return to an emphasis on the audile-tactile part of our sensorium that he suggests involves the interplay of all our senses. McLuhan is suggesting that with electric media one has an experience of synesthesia. "Electricity offers a means of getting in touch with every facet of being at once, like the brain itself. Electricity is only incidentally visual and auditory; it is primarily tactile (ibid., 219)." "The TV image requires each instant that we 'close' the spaces in the mesh by a convulsive sensuous participation that is profoundly kinetic and tactile, because tactility is the interplay of the senses, rather than the isolated contact of skin and object (ibid., 273)."

McLuhan argued that in acoustic space that we receive signals from all directions all at once, auditory signals by the ear in the oral tradition and electric/electromagnetic signals from all directions from all across the globe more or less simultaneously. He therefore extended his notion of acoustic space from the oral tradition to the electric age even though the signals in the electric age are not always auditory.

In the article "Art as Survival in the Electric Age," McLuhan (2005a, 213) explained that: "One of the peculiarities of the electric age is that we live simultaneously in all the cultures of the past. All of the past is here and all of the future is here."

McLuhan explained the connection between electric and auditory information as far back as 1957 in Volume 7 of the journal *Explorations*.

> The manuscript reader went too slowly, traveled too little to develop much time sense. Whatever of the past was discussed was felt as present, just as today the simultaneity and inclusiveness of our historical knowledge makes it all felt as being now. We have arrived once more at the oral via what appears as non-auditory means (McLuhan 2016, 99).

> Acoustic space in the oral tradition is about the simultaneity of auditory information, which parallels the simultaneity of electric information. And this is why McLuhan proposed that electrically configured information is acoustic in nature. Acoustic space is not only auditory but also tactile and even visual in the case of television. Acoustic space engages multiple senses whereas visual space only involves the eye (McLuhan 1969a).

Comparing Acoustic Space and Visual Space

Electricity reversed many aspects of the literary age so that there was a transition from fragmentation to integration, from centralization to decentralization and from an emphasis on hardware and the assembly line to one on software and learning as the following quote from *Understanding Media* indicates: "The restructuring of work and association was shaped by the techniques of fragmentation, that is the essence of machine technology (McLuhan 1964, 8)."

Visual and acoustic spaces were a key component of McLuhan's GToM. McLuhan characterized visual space as linear, sequential, one thing at a time, continuous and connected as opposed to the non-linear, simultaneous, discrete and disconnected nature of acoustic space. The linear sequential characteristics of the written word increased first with the introduction of alphabetic writing as opposed to ideographic writing and even more so with the printing press.

> The alphabet had the mysterious and unique power of separating the visual faculty from the other senses and giving dominant play to the visual. The pervasive use of uniform elements, the phonetic letters that the alphabet entailed, encouraged the additional visual matching of situational elements which formed the ground for Greek logic, geometry, and rationality. The idea of truth itself, the correspondence of thing and intellect, is based on matching (McLuhan and Logan 1977).

McLuhan maintained that orality and literacy have their respective acoustic and visual biases of communication and perception. "Rural Africans live largely in a world of sound – a world loaded with direct personal significance for the hearer – whereas the Western European lives much more in a visual world which is on the whole indifferent to him (McLuhan 1962, 28)."

Acoustic space is not only aural and oral but it is also tactile and includes the interplay of each of these senses. This space makes a direct contact with reality and its thought patterns are concrete. Much use is made of analogy and metaphor in acoustic space. In contrast visual space is a world of abstraction and deductive logic. It is where geometry and science live as opposed to art and music, which inhabit acoustic space. Visual space is characterized by linear, sequential, rational, fragmented, abstract, specialized and causal connections. Acoustic space, on the other hand, is concrete, inductive, simultaneous, intuitive, all-embracing, mystical and experiential. The patterns of visual space are primarily those of the left hemisphere of the brain while those of acoustic space are primarily associated with those of the right hemisphere. Given this division of the two hemisphere it is also the case that the left hemisphere is primarily focused on figure because it is linear, visual and analytic and the right hemisphere is focussed primarily on ground because it is acoustic and integrative. The use of the terms left and right hemisphere are more metaphorical than literal as we know that there is always participation of both hemispheres in all mental activities. For example, while a deficit in the left hemisphere leads to aphasia, a deficit in the right hemisphere affects the ability of a subject to understand metaphor or irony and they interpret language literally.

Unlike the visual and oral biases respectively of writing and speech, the biases of electric communication are not so obvious. According to McLuhan, however, electric information patterns are similar to those of oral communication because their integrative nature, their simultaneity, their decentralization and their lack of specialization (McLuhan 1962, 86). "A speed-up, such as occurs with electricity, may serve to restore a tribal pattern of intense involvement such as took place with the introduction of radio in Europe, and is now tending to happen as a result of TV in America. Specialist technologies detribalize. The non-specialist electric technology retribalizes (McLuhan 1964, 24)."

Here are some more comparisons of acoustic and visual space in McLuhan's own words.

"The alphabet, when pushed to a high degree of abstract visual intensity, became typography. The printed word with its specialist intensity bursts the bonds of medieval corporate guilds and monasteries, created extreme individualist patterns of enterprise and monopoly (McLuhan 1964, 23)."

"The separation of function and the division of stages, spaces and tasks are characteristic of literate and visual society and of the Western world. These divisions tend to dissolve through the action of the instant and organic interrelations of electricity (McLuhan 1964, 247)."

"Audile-tactile space is the space of involvement. We 'lose touch' without it. Visual space is the space of detachment and the public precautions we call 'scientific method' and scholarly or citational erudition (McLuhan 1964, 194–95)."

"Visual space is connected and creates detachment or non-involvement. It also tends to exclude the participation of the other senses (McLuhan 1995, 341)."

During an interview with the magazine Playboy McLuhan described acoustic space and contrasted it with visual space.

> [Acoustic] space that has no center and no margin, unlike strictly visual space, which is an extension and intensification of the eye. Acoustic space is organic and integral, perceived through the simultaneous interplay of all the senses; whereas "rational" or pictorial space is uniform, sequential and continuous and creates a closed world with none of the rich resonance of the tribal echoland. Our own Western time-space concepts derive from the environment created by the discovery of phonetic writing, as does our entire concept of Western civilization. The man of the tribal world led a complex, kaleidoscopic life precisely because the ear, unlike the eye, cannot be focused and is synesthetic rather than analytical and linear. Speech is an utterance, or more precisely, an outering, of all our senses at once; the auditory field is simultaneous, the

visual successive. The models of life of nonliterate people were implicit, simultaneous and discontinuous, and also far richer than those of literate man. By their dependence on the spoken word for information, people were drawn together into a tribal mesh; and since the spoken word is more emotionally laden than the written — conveying by intonation such rich emotions as anger, joy, sorrow, fear — tribal man was more spontaneous and passionately volatile. Audile-tactile tribal man partook of the collective unconscious, lived in a magical integral world patterned by myth and ritual, its values divine and unchallenged, whereas literate or visual man creates an environment that is strongly fragmented, individualistic, explicit, logical, specialized and detached (McLuhan 1969a).

McLuhan understood the transition from oral to written to electric communication in terms of the transition from acoustic space to visual space and back again to acoustic space. McLuhan (1962, 26) described the transition from the oral tradition to the written word with the one-liner, "man was given an eye for an ear," which also represented the transition from acoustic space to visual space. In the comparison of visual space and acoustic space it is the acoustic space that is ground-like and the visual space that is a figure-like. Information comes from all directions at once to the ear with oral communication and to the receiver with electric information which is why acoustic space is ground/environmental-like. Information in the literate age comes to the eye from a single direction so that visual space is figure-like as the information from a figure comes from a single direction.

Acoustic versus Visual Space and the Left/Right Split of the Brain

Towards the end of his career Marshall McLuhan began to think about the bicameral mind and the association of the left side of the brain with visual space and the right side of the brain with acoustic space. Although McLuhan's use of the bicameral mind literature was not an integral part of his GToM it provided comfort for him that his revolutionary ideas were correct and it also provided fodder to answer some of the bitter attacks of his critics. His mention of the bicameral mind appeared in his writings in only five places as far as I know beginning in 1976 in the following places:

- in the article Alphabet, Mother of Invention (McLuhan and Logan 1977) that he and I co-authored in 1976 and was not published until 1977;
- in a private letter written to Walter Ong in September of 1976 (https://mcluhangalaxy.wordpress.com/2016/02/17/an-unpublished-letter-from-marshall-mcluhan-to-father-walter-ong-sj-the-bicameral-mind/);

- in his book, *Laws of Media* (McLuhan, M. and E. McLuhan 1988), coauthored posthumously with his son Eric McLuhan and published in 1988;
- in an article entitled The Brain and Media: The "Western Hemisphere" (McLuhan 1988) published posthumously in the Antigonish Review in the summer of 1988; and
- in his book *Global Village: Transformations in World Life and Media in the 21st Century* coauthored posthumously with Bruce Powers and published in 1989 (McLuhan and Powers 1989).

These 5 items that were just reference emerged after I brought to McLuhan's attention the literature on the bicameral mind shortly after I start collaborating with him in 1974. I read a book on the bicameral mind that contained R. H. Trotter's diagram of the bicameral mind which also appears reprinted on page 68 of his book with his son, Eric, *The Laws of Media* (McLuhan, M. and E. McLuhan 1988, 68). The diagram associated the following characteristics of human thought with the left brain: logical, mathematical; linear, detailed; sequential; controlled; intellectual; dominant; worldly; active; analytic; reading, writing, naming; sequential ordering; perception of significant order; and complex motor sequences. Those characteristics associated with the right brain include: holistic; artistic, symbolic; simultaneous; emotional; intuitive, creative; minor (quiet); spiritual; receptive; synthetic, gestalt; facial recognition; simultaneous comprehension; perception of abstract patterns; and recognition of complex figures.

Although I cannot remember the title of the book it came from I have a vivid memory of the diagram itself because 2 or 3 days after lending Marshall the book in which it appeared he posted a large reproduction of the diagram above the door that led out of the room in which he worked in the Coach House that housed his Centre for Culture and Technology. He really latched on to the idea of the bicameral mind and he and I spend a great deal of time discussing it and eventually incorporating it into our article, Alphabet Mother of Invention (McLuhan and Logan 1977). Here is an excerpt from our article that deals with the left/right asymmetry of the brain:

Left-Right Split of the Brain and the Role of the Alphabet in Hemispheric Dominance

Recent developments in the field of neurophysiology tend to support the hypothesis that the alphabet produced a situation favorable for the development of logic, rational thought, and science.

Neurophysiologists have determined that while there is a certain degree of redundancy and overlap between the two hemispheres of the brain, essentially the left and right hemispheres of the brain perform specialized tasks. The right hemisphere is the locus of the artistic, intuitive, spiritual, holistic, simultaneous, discontinuous or creative side of our personalities, whereas the left hemisphere controls the lineal, visual, logical, analytic, mathematical, and verbal activities of our psyche.

We here suggest that the alphabet created a lineal and visual environment of services and experiences (everything from architecture and highways to representational art) which contributed to the ascendancy or dominance of the left, or lineal, hemisphere. This conjecture is consistent with the results of the Russian neurophysiologist Luria who found that the area of the brain which controls linear sequencing and, hence, logic, mathematics, and scientific thinking, is located in the prefrontal region of the left hemisphere:

The mental process for writing a word entails still another specialization: Putting the letters in the proper sequence to form the word. Lashley discovered many years ago that sequential analysis involved a zone of the brain different from that employed for spatial analysis. In the course of our extensive studies we have located the region responsible for sequential analysis in the anterior regions of the left hemisphere (Luria 1970).

Luria's results show that the expression "linear thinking" is not merely a figure of speech, but an actual, bona fide activity of the brain which takes place in the anterior regions of the left hemisphere of the brain. His results also indicate that the use of the alphabet, with its emphasis on linear sequence, stimulates this area of the brain. Luria's findings provide an understanding of how the written alphabet, with its lineal structure, was able to create the conditions conducive to the development of Western science, technology, and rationality.

The alphabet separated and isolated visual space from the many other kinds of sensory space involved in the senses of smell, touch, kinesthesia, and acoustics. This made possible the awareness of Euclidean space which is lineal, homogeneous, connected, and static. When neurophysiologists assign a vague "spatial" property to the right hemispheres they are referring to the simultaneous and discontinuous properties of audile-tactile and multiple other spaces of the sensorium. The Euclidean space of analytic geometry is a concept of the left hemisphere of the brain, while the multidimensional spaces of the holistic sensorium are precepts of the right hemisphere of the brain (McLuhan and Logan 1977).

Even more telling of the importance of the bicameral mind to McLuhan's thinking was the following letter he sent to Walter Ong in September of 1976:

> *The enclosures may help you to follow my work more easily. For thirty years at least, I have been using the two hemispheres approach under the names of the 'written' and the 'oral', the*

'visual' and the 'acoustic', the 'hot' and the 'cool, the 'medium' and the 'message, 'figure' and 'ground,' and so on. Now it turns out that medicine has been building a great beach-head for this approach with its new understanding of the two hemispheres of the brain. If you look at the traits of the left hemisphere, you will discover the lineaments of the First world – the literate and industrial world – and, on the other hand, in the right hemisphere you will perceive the characteristics of the Third world – the world without the phonetic alphabet.

During the past century, while the knowledge of the two hemispheres has been growing, there has also been a new electronic milieu or environment which automatically pushes the right hemisphere into a more dominant position than it has held in the Western world since the invention of the phonetic alphabet. The two hemispheres naturally respond to the milieu or total surround in which people live and work. My work has been a dialogue between the two hemispheres in which the characteristics of the right hemisphere are given so much recognition that I have been unintelligible to the left hemisphere people. It happens that the left hemisphere people are completely out of touch with the results and the formal characteristics of their own new electric technologies (McLuhan's unpublished letter to Walter Ong dated September 3, 1976 in the Walter J. Ong Archive at Saint Louis University and accessed June 19, 2019 on https://mcluhangalaxy.wordpress.com/2016/02/17/an-unpublished-letter-from-marshall-mcluhan-to-father-walter-ong-sj-the-bicameral-mind/*).*

The importance of this letter for me is that it provides support for the thesis that I am proposing in this study, namely, that McLuhan's ideas of *"written"* and the *"oral,"* the *"visual"* and the *"acoustic,"* the *"hot"* and the *"cool,"* the *"medium"* and the *"message, as well as "figure" and "ground," are all interconnected.*

Here are three quotes from McLuhan's posthumously published works where he once again invokes the idea of the bicameral mind.

From: *Laws of Media: The New Science*

Visual space is the result of left-hemisphere dominance in a culture, and its use is restricted to those cultures that have immersed themselves in the phonetic alphabet and thereby suppressed the activity of the right hemisphere. Since, as Jeremy Campbell points out in Grammatical Man, alphabetic consonants and much of syntax are products of the left hemisphere, visual space is an extrapolation into the environment of the left brain in high definition - abstract, structured as a figure minus a ground. Acoustic space has the basic character of a dynamic sphere whose focus or center is simultaneously everywhere and whose margin or periphery is nowhere. As it is multisensory, involving both the interval of tactility and kinetic equilibrium-pressure, it is one of the many figure/ground right-hemisphere forms of space … The alphabet created visual space, and with it a lineal and visual "outer world" environment of services and experiences (everything from architecture and highways to representational art), which contributed to the ascendancy or dominance of the left, or lineal, hemisphere. (McLuhan, M. and E. McLuhan 1988, 70 & 73).

From: The Brain and Media: The "Western Hemisphere"

> Because the dominant feature of the left hemisphere is linearity and sequentiality, there are good reasons for calling it the "visual" (quantitative) side of the brain; and because of the dominant features of the right hemisphere are simultaneous, holistic and synthetic, there are good reasons for indicating it as the "acoustic" (qualitative) side of the brain (McLuhan 1988).

From: *The Global Village: Transformations in World Life and Media in the 21ⁱˢᵗ Century.*

> The tetrad as a right-hemisphere visualization, helps us to see both figure and ground at a time when the latent effects of the mechanical age tend to obscure the ground subliminally. Its chief is that it raises the hidden ground to visibility enabling the analyst to perceive the double action of the visual (left hemisphere) and the acoustic (right hemisphere) in the life of the artifact or the idea. As such, the tetrad performs the function of myth in that it compresses past, present, and future into one through the power of simultaneity. The tetrad illumines the borderline between acoustic and visual space as an arena of spiraling repetition and replay, both of input and feedback, interlace and interface in the area of imploded circle of rebirth and metamorphosis (McLuhan and Powers 1989, 54).

McLuhan made a connection between the left and right hemispheres and figure and ground such that the right hemisphere is more aware of the ground than the left hemisphere and visa-versa the left hemisphere is more aware of figure than the right hemisphere.

(8) The Global Village

"Today, after more than a century of electric technology, we have extended our central nervous system itself in a global embrace, abolishing both space and time as far as our planet is concerned (McLuhan 1964, 3)."

> The electro-magnetic discoveries have re-created the simultaneous 'field' in all human affairs so that the human family now exists under conditions of a 'global village'. We live in a single constricted space resonant with tribal drums ... The new electronic interdependence recreates the world in the image of a global village (McLuhan 1962, 31).

McLuhan's notion of the Global Village, a term that he coined in his book *The Gutenberg Galaxy* in the quote above, is a key element of his GToM. He made use of the term in many of his works. Whether or not it is a coincidence it is interesting to note that the term "globalization" was first used in 1959 a couple of years before McLuhan coined the expression "the global village." Ironically, the term "the global village" has entered the English language to such a degree that more people are familiar with the expression than they are with McLuhan's name.

The idea of the global village is perhaps McLuhan's grandest reversal of all when you consider that what he was basically suggesting is that the whole planet reverses into a village.

In his book *The Medium is the Massage* McLuhan and Fiore wrote:

> Ours is a brand-new world of all-at-once-ness. 'Time' has ceased, 'space' has vanished. We now live in a global village ... a simultaneous happening ... The new electronic interdependence recreates the world in the image of a global village. Positively, the effect of speeding up temporal sequence is to abolish time, much as the telegraph and cable abolished space (McLuhan & Fiore 1968, 63).

In an article written in 1963 and republished in 1996 McLuhan wrote:

> Post-literate man's electronic media contract the world to a village or tribe where everything happens to everyone at the same time: everyone knows about, and therefore participates in, everything that is happening the minute it happens. Television gives this simultaneity to events in the global village (McLuhan 1996a).

The Internet has played an important role in the realization of McLuhan's vision of a global village.

> Electricity [and the Internet] bringing information instantaneously from the four corners of the planet invests distant events with a personal dimension; it is as though they are occurring in one's own community. Communities across the globe become entwined in one another's affairs. Electrically based media transform the role of the individual in society. A social grid of highly independent individuals gives way to tribal patterns of intense involvement with one another and a return to elements of the oral tradition. McLuhan pushes Innis' (1951 & 1972) notion of light media providing command over space to its limit when considering the impact of telecommunication in which information travels at the speed of light. The command over space reduces the entire globe to the dimensions of a village - a "global village" (Logan 2004, 46).

I sometimes regard the Internet as a de facto global village. Perhaps this is too much of an exaggeration but it certainly is the case that it operates as the town crier of the global village because of the way it brings us all together. As McLuhan pointed out, however, all technologies provide service and disservice so it is obvious that digital technologies also discourage face to face communication, an important element of village life.

A key element in McLuhan's historical overview of communications is that electric information moving at the velocity of light creates new patterns of communication and social interactions. He describes this as "an instant implosion" that reverses the specialism of the literary age and contracted the globe to a village in which "everybody lives in the utmost proximity created by our electric involvement in one another's lives" (McLuhan 1964, 35).

Many have interpreted McLuhan's notion of the global village as a place of harmony. He, in fact, felt the exact opposite. "The global village is a world in which you don't necessarily have harmony, you have extreme concern with everybody else's business, and much involvement in everybody else's life (https://www.cbc.ca/mcluhan/mashup-challenge/about.html, accessed July 24, 2020)."

> The closer you get together, the more you like each other? There's no evidence of that in any situation that we've ever heard of. When people get close together, they get more and more savage, impatient with each together …. The global village is a place of very arduous interfaces and very abrasive situations … (from an interview on *The Education of Mike McManus*, TV Ontario December 28, 1977)

> Of all the developments of electric based information systems perhaps none has contributed more to the creation of a global village than the Internet and the World Wide Web. Information arrives on our desktop from all over the planet taking essentially no more time to arrive from halfway around the globe than from a next-door neighbor's Web site. Not only has the time barrier been eliminated but so too has the cost barrier, if one has made the investment of a computer and paid for a link to the Internet. There are still North-South issues in that there is not an equal, or for that matter, equitable distribution of communication and computing capabilities in our global village but with the ongoing reduction in the cost of computing and communications hopefully these disparities will disappear in the not too distant future.

(9) Media as Environment and Media Ecology

McLuhan regarded media as environments as the following quotes indicate: "Any understanding of social and cultural change is impossible without a knowledge of the way media work as environments (McLuhan and Fiore 1967, 26)." "Any new technology, any extension or amplification of human faculties given material embodiment, tends to create a new environment (McLuhan 2005b, Vol. 4, 6)." "It is perfectly clear to me that all media are environment (McLuhan 1970a, 4)."

Given that media are environments it follows that the study of media environments would be the ecology of media or simply media ecology just as the study of environments is known as ecology. The term media ecology was first introduced by Neil Postman in 1968 according to the Wikipedia article Media Ecology:

Media ecology theory is the study of media, technology, and communication and how they affect human environments. The theoretical concepts were proposed by Marshall McLuhan in 1964, while the term *media ecology* was first formally introduced by Neil Postman in 1968 (https://en.wikipedia.org/wiki/Media_ecology, accessed July 5, 2019).

Although perhaps Marshall McLuhan was not the first to use the term "media ecology" the concept is an integral part of his GToM as he regarded media as environment as we just mentioned. In a 1955 article he (McLuhan 1955) spoke of media as though they were Darwinian species. Given his use of this biological metaphor, the study of media, is therefore media ecology. He understood that media were constantly interacting with each other and undergoing constant change. This is clear from the following passage in that 1955 article:

> The media can be viewed as artificial extensions of our sensory existence–each medium an externalized species, as it were, of the inner genus sensation. The cultural environment created by the externalizations of the modes of sensation now favors the predominance of one sense or another, and these species struggle through various mutations in a desperate attempt at adaptation and survival (McLuhan 1955).

McLuhan (1962, 7) in the *Gutenberg Galaxy* wrote: "Any technology tends to create a new human environment … Technological environments are not merely passive containers of people but are active processes that reshape people and other technologies alike." He again returns to this biological/ecological perspective in 1964 in *Understanding Media*. "No medium has its meaning or existence alone, but only in constant interplay with other media (McLuhan 1964, 39)." "A new medium is never an addition to an old one, nor does it leave the old one in peace. It never ceases to oppress the older media until it finds new shapes and positions for them (McLuhan 1964, 158)."

The point that McLuhan was making is that media and technologies interact with each other and together with their users to form an ecosystem, which is the essence of media ecology. He even made explicit use of the term ecology in two of his earlier writings dating back to 1970:

> The electric age is the age of **ecology**. It is the study and projection of the total environments or organisms and people, because of the instant coherence of all factors, made possible by moving information at electric speeds (McLuhan & Parker 1970, 36, bolding mine).

> It is perfectly clear to me that all media are environments. As environments, all media have all the effects that geographers and biologists have associated with environments in the past … The medium is the message because the environment transforms our perceptions governing the areas of attention and neglect alike … The absence of

interest in causation cannot persist in the new age of **ecology**. **Ecology** does not seek connections, but patterns. It does not seek quantities, but satisfactions and understanding (McLuhan 1970a, 4; bolding mine).

Another indication of McLuhan's ecological approach was his interest in field theory and a general systems approach as early as 1953: "All types of linear approaches to situations past, present, or future are useless. Already in the sciences there is recognition of the need for a unified field theory, general systems theory: which enable scientists to use one continuous set of terms by way of relating the various scientific universes (McLuhan 1953, 126)."

The only evidence I could find of McLuhan using the term media ecology was in our book *The Future of the Library: From Electric Media to Digital Media* (Logan and McLuhan 2016). However, his constant use of the term environment to describe media implied the notion of media ecology especially in the context of this 1967 comment, "Environments are not just containers, but are processes that change the content totally (McLuhan 1966, 200)." We will grant that perhaps the term of media ecology was coined by Neil Postman and later adopted by McLuhan, but I believe it is clear that the origin of the concept lies with McLuhan who is responsible for the biological spin he gave to media theory and what is now called media ecology. Although many credit Postman with the first use of the term out of respect for my friend Eric McLuhan of blessed memory I need to report his claim that during his visit and that of his father's to Fordham in New York City in the fall of 1967 that he was using the term media ecology before Postman. There is no way of verifying his claim but certainly the first published use of the term belongs to Postman as well as its popularization through his founding of the Media Ecology Program at New York University.

(10) The Laws of Media (LoM)

McLuhan developed a set of rules, which he called the Laws of the Media (LoM) or the tetrad, as they are sometimes referred to in the literature (McLuhan 1975, 1977; McLuhan, M. and McLuhan, E. 1988). The LoM were a tool he used for studying the effects of media and all forms of human artifacts, which specifically illustrate their counterintuitive nature.

The Laws of Media (LoM) for studying the counterintuitive effects of media, or technologies, scientific laws or any human-made artifact consists of the following four law:

(1) Every medium, technology or human-made artifact enhances some human function.
(2) In doing so, it obsolesces some former medium, technology, or human-made artifact, which was used to achieve the same function earlier.
(3) In achieving its function, the new medium, technology or human-made artifact retrieves some older form from the past that has been obsolesced.
(4) And when pushed far enough, the new medium, technology or human-made artifact reverses or flips into a complementary or possibly an opposite form.

To illustrate a LoM, let us first consider the medium of money, which enhances trade and commerce, obsolesces the barter system, retrieves the conspicuous consumption of hunting and gathering societies, and flips into credit. Or consider the technology of the automobile, which enhances transportation, obsolesces the horse and carriage, retrieves the knight in shining armor, and flips into the traffic jam, that is, the lack of mobility (Marshall McLuhan private communication).

The laws apply with equal validity to all the artifacts of humankind, whether they are communication media, technologies, or scientific laws or principles. The term "obsolescence" used in this context requires some clarification because the word is often misinterpreted or interpreted too literally. The obsolescence of the barter system by money does not mean that the use of cash forever ended the straight exchange of commodities. It does mean, however, that cash transactions became the dominant mode of commercial exchange. Similarly, the obsolescence of the horse and carriage did not end forever this mode of transportation, which is still used as a tourist attraction in large cities and as a mode of transport in many third-world centers or among certain cultural groups such as the Mennonites. The automobile, however, has come to dominate traffic patterns.

The point that obsolescence does not mean the eradication of a medium but rather the end of its dominance is something that becomes particularly important when considering the obsolescence of print by electric information. When McLuhan indicated that electricity had obsolesced print, defenders of the book pointed to statistics that showed an increase in the sale of books and the number of new titles available. They argued that the book had not been obsolesced but was alive and well. What these critics failed to grasp is that electric information has come to dominate print as the principal mode of distributing information and that the information consumers spend far more time with is electric or electronic media such as radio, television and computers than they do with books. They also failed to consider that the production of print material was also being more and more influenced by the electronic telecommunication, handling, and storage of information. When writing obsolesced the oral tradition, people did not suddenly stop talking to each other. But writing came to dominate the spoken word whenever a permanent record of information was desired or communication over distance was required. A technology or medium does not disappear when it becomes obsolesced; it still exists but it no longer dominates the human function it once performed and enhanced. "Obsolescence never meant the end of anything, it's just the beginning (McLuhan 2010, 139)." "Likewise, when print obsolesced handwriting, handwritten communication was not completely wiped out it just played second fiddle to print. Although most recorded music is digital the analog vinyl record is still very much alive (Logan 2011)." McLuhan and I suggested that eBooks would not obsolesce the printed book.

> In industry there is an old saying: "If it works, it is obsolete." We have been saying that the book and printing are obsolete, for some years. Many people interpret this to mean that printing and the book are about to disappear. Obsolescence, in fact, means the exact opposite. It means that a service has become so pervasive that it permeates every area of a culture like the vernacular itself. Obsolescence, in short, ensures total acceptance and ever wider use (Logan and McLuhan 2016).

When we apply the Laws of the Media to the various forms of electric technology one of the recurring themes of the reversal will be the flip into information overload. Each new medium that arises is trying to cope with the information overload created by the media that preceded it. In a radio interview in 1967 on the Canadian Broadcasting Company McLuhan explained this effect. "One of the effects of living with electric information is that we live habitually in a state of information overload. There's always more than you can cope with."

The Laws of the Media (LoM) are a tool to probe the effects of a medium, tool or technology. The four laws of the LoM differ from a physics law in the sense that it does not make a unique prediction as to what is retrieved from the past or what complementary form the technology or medium will flip into. There might be several things retrieved from the past. The LoM is a generalization or laws that describes the same general pattern of enhancement, obsolescence, retrieval and reversal that all media obey. The LoM is an exploratory tool or probe that provides insights into the effects that a medium or technology creates and how it might evolve.

To obtain some insight into the usefulness of the LoM and since LoM are a human artifact, we can apply the LoM analysis to McLuhan's Laws of Media. What does LoM enhance, obsolesce, retrieve and flip into. Well, LoM enhance our understanding of human artifacts that the LoM are applied to. They obsolesce considering artifacts strictly as figures minus the ground or the environment in which they operate. They retrieve ecology and systems thinking and pushed far enough LoM flip into the reversal of cause and effect, media ecology and as I am suggesting McLuhan's GToM.

While the LoM are an interesting and useful tool, they do not by any means describe McLuhan's GToM. They do contain some of the elements of the GToM in that enhancement, retrieval, obsolescence, and reversal (or flip) all play a role in McLuhan's understanding of media.

Conclusion: McLuhan's GToM was the Underlying Basis for his Predictions and his Understanding of Media and their Impacts

Given that McLuhan was able to foreshadow or predict so much of the phenomena of the digital age many years before they emerged indicates that he obviously must have been working from a theoretical basis which I claim is the GToM described in this chapter. One cannot make so many accurate predictions without having a theoretical framework to work from.

I believe that we have established that McLuhan's GToM is in large part based on reversals with the primary ones being the reversals of figure and ground; concepts and percepts; cause and effects; and visual and acoustic space. I have listed others in Chapter Six.

I believe that we have only scratched the surface in describing McLuhan's General Theory of Media but hopefully I have demonstrated that the figure/ground dichotomy and the many reversals he identified played an essential role in his GToM. I also believe that given so many of McLuhan's prediction proved to be accurate years after he made them that his theory is in the same class as the theories of Newton, Darwin, Freud, Einstein and Pavlov, the scientists with whom Tom Wolfe compared McLuhan.

McLuhan identified media and technologies as "extensions of man" that act as a form enabling a force that effects the human psyche and human institutions. This parallels Newton's identification of force as the source of acceleration in mechanics, Freud's identification of unconscious and suppressed memories as the force that drives human behavior, Darwin's identification of natural selection as the process that enables the force that drives evolution, Pavlov's identification of conditioning as the procedure enabling the force that drives animal behavior and Einstein's identification of space-time and relativity as the new concepts replacing the mechanics and gravity of Newton as the prime force of matter over large distances.

References

Bertalanffy, Ludwig von. *General System Theory: Foundations, Development, Applications.* New York: George Braziller, revised edition 1976, 1968.

Carpenter, Edmund. *Eskimo.* Toronto: University of Toronto Press (originally was Volume 9 of *Explorations: Studies in Culture and Communication*), 1959.

Culkin, John. "A Schoolman's Guide to Marshall McLuhan." *Saturday Review* 51–53 (March 18, 1967): 71–72.

Eliade, Mircea. *Patterns in Comparative Religion.* New York: Sheed & Ward, 1958.

Findlay-White, Emma, and Robert K. Logan. "Acoustic Space, Marshall McLuhan and Links to Medieval Philosophers and Beyond: Center Everywhere and Margin Nowhere." *MDPI Philosophies* 1, no. 2 (2016): 162–69.

Frazer, Sir James. *The Golden Bough.* London: Macmillan and Co, 1890.

Havelock, Eric. *Preface to Plato.* Cambridge, MA: Harvard University Press, 1963.

Innis, Harold. *The Bias of Communication.* Toronto: University of Toronto Press, 1951.

Innis, Harold. *Empire and Communications.* With foreword by Marshall McLuhan. Originally published by Oxford University Press [1950]. Toronto: University of Toronto Press, 1972.

Karadzic, Vuk Stefanovic. *Works.* Belgrade, 1972.

Levinson, Paul. *Digital McLuhan: A Guide to the Information Millennium.* Abington-on-Thames: Routledge, 1999.

Logan, Robert K. "The Five Ages of Communication." *Explorations in Media Ecology* 1: 13–20, 2002.

Logan, Robert K. "Science as a Language, the Non-Probativity Theorem and the Complementarity of Complexity and Predictability." In *Humanity and the Cosmos*, edited by Daniel McArthur and Cory Mulvihill. Binghamton, NY: Global Academic Publishing, 63–73, 2003.

Logan, Robert K. *The Alphabet Effect: A Media Ecology Understanding of the Making of Western Civilization.* Cresskill, NJ: Hampton Press (1st edition 1986. New York: Wm. Morrow), 2004.

Logan, Robert K. "McLuhan Misunderstood: Setting the Record Straight." *International Journal of McLuhan Studies* 1: 27–47, 2011.

Logan, Robert K. *Understanding New Media: Extending Marshall McLuhan*, 2nd Ed. New York: Peter Lang Publishing (1st Edition 2010. New York: Peter Lang), 2016.

Logan, Robert K. *Understanding Man: The Extensions of Digital Media*, https://www.researchgate.net/publication/313601251_Understanding_Man_The_Extensions_of_Digital_Media, 2018.

Logan, Robert K., and Marshall McLuhan. *The Future of the Library: From Electric Media to Digital Media.* New York: Peter Lang Publishing, 2016.

Lord, Albert. *The Singer of Tales.* Cambridge, MA: Harvard University Press, 1960.

Luria, A. R. "The Functional Organization of the Brain." *Scientific American* 222, no. 3 (1970): 66–78.

Marchand, Philip. *Marshall McLuhan: The Medium and the Messenger*. Toronto: Random House, 1989.
McLuhan, Marshall. "Not for Children." *Exploration* 1 (1953): 117–27.
McLuhan, Marshall. "Communication and Communication Art: A Historical Approach to the Media." *Teachers College Record* 57, no. 2 (1955): 104–10.
McLuhan, Marshall. *The Gutenberg Galaxy: The Making of Typographic Man*. Toronto: University of Toronto Press, 1962.
McLuhan, Marshall. *Understanding Media: Extensions of Man*. New York: McGraw Hill, 1964. (The page references in the text are for the McGraw Hill paperback second edition. Readers should be aware that the pagination in other editions is different.)
McLuhan, Marshall. "Address at Vision 65." *American Scholar* 35 (spring 1966): 196–205.
McLuhan, Marshall. "Casting my Perils before Swains." In *McLuhan Hot and Cool*, edited by Gerard Emanuel Stearn. New York: Dial Press, 1967.
McLuhan, Marshall. "Include Me Out: The Reversal of the Overheated Image." *Playboy* 15, no. 12 (December, 1968): 61–64, 245.
McLuhan, Marshall. "Playboy Magazine Interview." *Playboy* 16, no. 3 (March, 1969): 53–74, 158.
McLuhan, Marshall. *Counterblast*. New York: Harcourt, Brace and World, 1969b.
McLuhan, Marshall. "Education in the Electronic Age." *Interchange* 1, no. 4 (1970a): 1–12.
McLuhan, Marshall. "Living in an Acoustic World." (http://www.marshallmcluhanspeaks.com/lecture/1970-living-in-an-acoustic-world/?t=09m14s. Accessed April 20, 2019), 1970b.
McLuhan, Marshall. "Marshall McLuhan Convocation Address, The University of Alberta." http://projects.chass.utoronto.ca/mcluhan-studies/v1_iss5/1_5art3.htm. Accessed April 16, 2019, 1971.
McLuhan, Marshall. "The Future of the Book." In *Understanding Me: Lectures & Interviews*, edited by Stephanie McLuhan & David Staines. Toronto: McClelland & Stewart, 1972.
McLuhan, Marshall. "Communication: McLuhan's Laws of Media." *Technology and Culture* 16, no. 1 (1975): 74–78.
McLuhan, Marshall. "The User is Content." *Tomorrow Show with Tom Snyder*, NBC, September 6, 1976 (https://en.wikiquote.org/wiki/Marshall_McLuhan. Accessed April 15, 2019), 1976.
McLuhan, Marshall. "Laws of Media." *English Journal* 67, no. 8 (1977): 92–94. Also published *Et Cetera* 34, no. 2: 173–79.
McLuhan, Marshall. "Living at the Speed of Light." *Maclean's Magazine* (January 7, 1980): 32–33.
McLuhan, Marshall. "The Brain and Media: The 'Western Hemisphere'". *Antigonish Review* 74–75 (1988): 182–96.
McLuhan, Marshall. "The Emperor's New Clothes." In *Essential McLuhan*, edited by Eric McLuhan and Frank Zingrone. Concord Ontario: Anansi, 1995.
McLuhan, Marshall. "The Agenbite of Outwit." McLuhan Studies Issue 2 (Can be accesses at http://projects.chass.utoronto.ca/mcluhan-studies/v1_iss2/1_2art6.htm), 1996a.
McLuhan, Marshall. *Forward Through the Rearview Mirror*. Toronto: Prentice Hall, 1996b.

McLuhan, Marshall. "Art as Survival in the Electric Age." In *Understanding Me: Lectures and Interviews*, edited by Stephanie McLuhan and David Staines. Cambridge, MA: MIT Press, 2005a.

McLuhan, Marshall. *Marshall McLuhan Unbound*, Vol. 4, edited by W. Terrence Gordon. Corte Madera, CA: Gingko Press, 2005b.

McLuhan, Marshall. *The Medium and the Light: Reflections on Religion and Media*. Eugene, OR: Wipf & Stock Pub, 2010.

McLuhan, Marshall. "The Effect of the Printed Book on Language in the 16th Century." In *Explorations: Studies in Culture and Communication*, Vol. 7, edited by Edmund Carpenter and Marshall McLuhan. Eugene, OR: Wipf & Stock Pub, 2016.

McLuhan, Marshall, and Quentin Fiore. *The Medium is the Massage: An Inventory of Effects*. New York: Random House, 1967.

McLuhan, Marshall, and Quentin Fiore. *War and Peace in the Global Village*. New York: Simon & Shuster, 1968.

McLuhan, Marshall, and Harley Parker. *Counterblast*. London: Rapp and Whiting, 1970.

McLuhan, Marshall, and Barrington Nevitt. *Take Today: The Executive as Dropout*. Toronto: Longman Canada, 1972.

McLuhan, Marshall, and Robert K. Logan. "Alphabet, Mother of Invention." *Et Cetera* 34, no. 4 (1977): 373–83.

McLuhan, Marshall, and Eric McLuhan. *Laws of Media: The New Science*. Toronto: University of Toronto Press, 1988.

McLuhan, Marshall, and Bruce R. Powers. *The Global Village: Transformations in World Life and Media in the 21st Century*. New York: Oxford University Press, 1989.

McLuhan, Marshall, and David Carson. *The Book of Probes*. Corte Madera, CA: Gingko Press, 2003.

McLuhan, Marshall, and Eric McLuhan. *Media and Formal Cause*. New York: NeoPoiesis Press, 2011.

Molinaro, Matie, Corrine McLuhan, and William Toye (eds). *Letters of Marshall McLuhan*. Toronto: Oxford University Press, 1987.

Ong, Walter. *Ramus, Method, and the Decay of Dialogue; from the Art of Discourse to the Art of Reason*. Cambridge, MA: Harvard University Press, 1958.

Parry, Millman. Millman Parry Collection of Oral Literature On-line. (https://mpc.chs.harvard.edu//. Accessed June 16, 2019).

Popper, Karl. *The Logic of Scientific Discovery* (originally written in German as Logik der Forschung). London: Routledge, 1959.

Strate, Lance. *Media Ecology: An Approach to Understanding the Human Condition*. New York: Peter Lang Publishing, 2017.

Theall, Donald. *The Virtual Marshall McLuhan*. Montreal & Kingston: McGill-Queen's University Press, 2001.

CHAPTER THREE

Applying McLuhan's General Theory of Media to the Flowering of the Digital Age

Introduction

McLuhan made use of reversals in the formulation of his General Theory of Media (GToM) as was documented in Chapters One and Two. It was suggested that McLuhan's focus on reversals can be traced back to his encounter with electric technology and the transition from written to electric communication. McLuhan himself pointed out that this transition from mechanical forms to electric ones was characterized by many reversals from the explosion of the mechanical era to the implosion of the electric one.

Just as the transition from written to electric communication created many reversals, the same is happening with the transition we are living through now, namely, the transition from electric-based to digital-based communication. McLuhan did not witness this transition because of his incapacitating stroke in 1979 and his passing in 1980. The principal digital media that existed at this time were main frame and mini computers. The personal computer (PC) revolution was just getting under way at the end of McLuhan's career and he had little or no direct contact with these developments. Although mainframe and minicomputers had significant impacts on social, economic and political systems they had considerably less impact than that of personal computers, the Internet, the Web, smartphones, and AI, the media that are at the heart of the digital revolution almost all of which emerged after McLuhan's passing. The reason that the main frame and mini computers did not have the same impact as personal computers is that mainframes and minis were not being used by the general public and their impacts were largely confined to business, government, the military and academe. We therefore regard the threshold for the reversal of the electric age into the digital age as the emergence of the personal computer circa 1980. The digital age really took off, however, in 1994 with the release of Netscape, the first publicly accessible Web browser, and the public use of the Internet and the World Wide Web.

The focus of this chapter will be to understand the reversals that occurred as we passed from the electric age to the digital age. A second focus is to extend McLuhan's GToM to enrich our understanding of digital media drawing, in particular, on his Laws of Media. First, we will examine the impacts of mainframe frame and mini computers that existed at the time McLuhan was active, keeping in mind that he did not have first-hand knowledge of these technologies as a user. Next, we will examine all of the new media and services of the digital age that emerged after McLuhan's passing looking at each of these developments in the context of McLuhan reversals and his Laws of Media.

Main Frame and Mini Computers

The impact of mainframe and mini computers resulted in the automation of many mechanical-like activities by speeding up the time to complete these tasks. McLuhan and Nevitt (1973, 10) pointed this out in their description of the use of computers in their times: "*Computers are still serving* as agents to sustain pre-computer effects." This is consistent with McLuhan's view that a new technology is used at first only to achieve what the old technologies had achieved but in a more efficient way: "It is part of the age-old habit of using new means for old purposes instead of discovering what are the new goals contained in the new means (McLuhan 1970c, 202)." He expressed a similar thought when he wrote, "Our typical response to disrupting new technology is to recreate the old environment instead of heeding the new opportunities of the new environment (McLuhan 1997b, 113)."

> The new opportunities that McLuhan spoke of did not surface until the emergence and wide spread use of personal computers in the late 70's and the Internet in the 90's and in particular the use of the World Wide Web that went public in 1994 with the release of the Internet browser Netscape. To illustrate why I claim mainframe computers pre-Internet had a certain mechanical aspect to them and were not as simultaneous as today's computers connected to the Internet let me share with you, the readers, an episode from my use of the mainframe computer at MIT in the mid 60's.

As a grad student engaged in elementary particle physics research circa 1963–65, I made use of the MIT main frame computer to carry out numerical analyses comparing a current theory at the time, Regge poles, with experimental data. I first had to first write a program using Fortran IV. The program together with the data I was analyzing was then entered into the mainframe computer using punched hole cards prepared on a special machine with a typewriter-like keyboard. The deck of cards holding the program and the data, were then submitted as a batch job along with other batch jobs for the mainframe operators to process. The results of the computation were available the next day printed on large sheets of paper. I would then study the output and prepare the next phase of the calculation I wanted to make.

Frequently, the actual calculation I wanted the computer to make did not take place because I made a stupid error in preparing my punched card inputs. I might have forgotten a single comma in a crucial place, for example. Whenever this happened I had to correct the mistake and resubmit my deck and hope there were no other mistakes in my deck because each time my deck was rejected I lost a day. This procedure was far from simultaneous and there was a mechanical aspect to conducting my numerical analysis of the experimental data using the mainframe computer. And then there was the day I clumsily spilled my box of punched cards on the floor and there was another day was gone, as I laboriously re-assembled my box of punched cards in their correct order. Using the mainframe computer at MIT was a slow and painful process. Towards the end of my project as I was putting the final touches on my thesis I given special permission to access to our mainframe computer in the middle of the night with an operator in attendance. This was an amazing experience at the time because I could see the results of my calculation in real time. I experienced in the middle of that night for 3 or 4 hours what it was like to have a personal computer 15 years before they became a reality. I was able to complete in those 3 or 4 hours what would have taken at least a month or two to complete.

The Personal Computer Revolution

Perhaps the most important aspect of the personal computer revolution was the way in which it democratized computing. In 1943 there were 5 computers in the world. In 2019 there are 4.536 billion users of the Internet (https://www.internetworldstats.com/stats.htm). The digital revolution begins with the emergence of the personal computer (PC). It would seem logical that a company like IBM that dominated the mainframe business would have been at the forefront of the PC revolution. But as McLuhan explained, IBM applied computing to the tasks of the previous environment of the mechanical era. In Chapter One we described how McLuhan in a conversation with IBM executives talked about a computer in every home which they dismissed as nonsense. The personal computer revolution was started by hackers and hobbyists and not the professionals that worked with mainframes at IBM and minis at DEC. The hobbyists built their own computers using readily available electronic components.

Steve Wozniak and Steve Jobs, the founders of Apple Computers, were typical of the PC revolutionaries. Before working with computers, they hacked pay phones to make long distance phone calls for free. They learned about computing on their own not as students at a university nor as the employees of a computer company like IBM. They were hobbyists. They worked out of the garage of the Job's family home. There they developed their first prototype the Apple I in 1976 which they sold for $666.66. They then used the profits of approximately $800,000 from this venture to develop the Apple II with which they entered the market in a serious and very successful way in 1977. The Apple II took the computer market by storm netting them $139 million in sales in the first 3 years of operation. The next step for Apple was the MacIntosh in 1984, the first computer with a graphic user interface (GUI) that took advantage of the user design genius of Jobs. They were not the first into the PC market but they enjoyed the success they achieved because of their focus on user design. They designed and developed their own hardware, operating system and software to create a totally integrated system, something IBM did not do when they finally got into the PC business in 1981.

IBM looking to its mainframe corporate customer base to sell their PC products failed to understand the potential PC market of a computer in every home as McLuhan had predicted when he met with a number of IBMers back in 1968. Perhaps in a hurry to get into the PC market IBM made the fatal mistake of farming out the development of their operating system and software to the fledgling Microsoft company headed by Bill Gates and their microchips manufacturing to Intel. They gave away the two most lucrative parts of the PC business to these two firms and by so doing undercut their PC business. After delivering to IBM the essential ingredients for a PC, Intel and Microsoft were only too glad to sell their products to other companies who created what were called PC clones, which did everything an IBM PC could do and at a cheaper price.

The only role that IBM played in the PC market was to manufacture and distribute personal computers primarily for their corporate customer base. Apple, on the other hand, went on to develop products and services that heeded "the new opportunities of the new environment" that McLuhan (1997b, 113) had spoken about. They went on to become the dominant player in the PC digital device and service arena and the very first company to achieve a market value of one trillion dollars. What they learned from the success of the Apple II and then the MacIntosh led to the development of a series of new products and services. They did not see themselves solely as a manufacturer and developer of personal computers but rather as a company that provided services and accessories related to their line of computers and other digital devices. They signaled their new stance when they changed their name in January of 2007 from Apple Computers Inc. to simply Apple Inc. Here is a list of their products and services that reflect the reason for the change of their name to Apple Inc.:

- Their hardware products: Mac Book Air and Pro; the iPod, a portable media player; the iPad tablet computer; the iPhone (not the first smart phone but one that dominated that sector); Apple Watch; Apple TV; and the HomePod smart speaker. Each of these had their own associated operating systems that were developed exclusively by Apple Inc.
- The stores, services and software apps they created that were married to their hardware products including: iTunes, iOS App Store, Mac App Store, Apple Music, Apple TV+, iMessage, iCloud, Safari web browser, iLife, iWork, Final Cut Pro, Logic Pro, Xcode, their retail outlets Apple Store and the associated Genius Bar, Apple Care, ApplePay, ApplePay Cash and Apple Card.

Although a number of these products or services were not the first of their kind, but they were the most elegantly designed in the market place and dominated each market that they entered.

The Digital Age of Hybridization and Interconnectedness

It was only with the emergence of personal computers in the late 1970s; the Net and the Web for public use in 1994; smartphones in 1999 and all that followed in their wake that the digital revolution began in full force. What we now call digital natives were those born beginning in 1990. Born in 1939, I began using mainframe computers in 1963 at the age of 24, I cannot consider myself a digital native. My son David, born in 1969, who reprogrammed our Apple 2 computer the first night we brought the device home in 1981 might be regarded as a digital native although the term usually refers to kids born after 1990 to differentiate them from adults like me, who were introduced to digital technologies for the first time as adults. For the sake of the discussion to be developed in this chapter we will regard the digital age and the digital revolution as commencing with personal computers and the Internet using 1977, the year the Apple II was released, as the approximate start date of the digital age. Although the mainframe and mini computers that began to appear in the early 1940s were digital, they did not have a universal impact as they were in the hands of technical specialists that represent a small percentage of the population. It is only with the personal computer that digital technology began to affect the general public.

One of the distinctions that McLuhan made between the ages of written and electric communication was that the technology of the former was mechanical, linear, sequential and visual while that of the latter was simultaneous, field-like and acoustic. Digital age technologies which incorporate electric age technologies are also simultaneous and acoustic like electric mass media but they have the additional property that they are interconnected and form hybrid systems to a much greater extent than electric mass media. Computers (PCs, minis and mainframes), tablets, smart phones, the Internet, email, texting, the World Wide Web, Web apps such as social media, etc. are all interconnected, integrated and taken together form a hybrid technological behemoth. If mechanical, linear and sequential captured the character of the literate age and simultaneous and field-like captures the character of the Electric Age, then hybrid and interconnected captures the character of the digital age. With my MacBook Pro and a wi-fi connection I can connect with so many different servers including the Cloud, access so many apps, enjoy so much multimedia and link up with so many other PCs with whom I share a connection vis-à-vis the Internet. My PC is part of an extremely complex hybrid extended and interconnected technological environment. In fact, one can consider the Internet, the Web, all the computers and servers connected to them, all their apps, all their content and all the peripheral devices connected to these computers and servers as one global hybrid technological device. I therefore suggest that hybridization and interconnectedness are the new features of the digital age that differentiate it from the electric age.

Another Aspect of Interconnectedness: Every Person as a Broadcaster

There is another aspect of the interconnectedness of digital media, which is that every user of a PC with an Internet connection becomes a broadcaster or perhaps at least a narrowcaster through their tweets, blogs, podcasts or social media sites. As pointed out in Chapter Two electric mass media operated in the broadcast mode where only a small number of organizations were able to disseminate their content by radio or television. This was also true of the owners of a printing press such as newspapers, magazines and book publishers who are able to disseminate their content in a broadcast mode. With the advent of photocopying McLuhan (1974) pointed out that "Gutenberg made everybody a reader. Xerox makes everybody a publisher." Riffing on McLuhan's quote I suggest that "Apple made everybody a computer operator. The Internet makes everybody a broadcaster."

The combination of the PC + the Internet provides users with a channel to create and communicate their content and as a result communication in the digital age is even more decentralized that was the case with electrically configured mass media. McLuhan's (1964, 47) observation that "electricity does not centralize but decentralizes" holds in the digital age to an even greater extent. But the decentralization is not complete given that the world of digital media is dominate by a small number of mega-monopolies, namely Facebook, Google, Apple, Microsoft and Amazon. During the era of electric communication there were still monopolies such as the television networks, ABC, CBS, and NBC is the U.S. and CBC and CTV in Canada which dominated TV totally until the arrival of cable TV. It is ironic, however that with the Internet and digital media that the five mega-monopolies we listed above dominate their markets even more than the TV networks. The first company to achieve a valuation of a trillion dollars was Apple followed closely by Amazon, Google (Alphabet), and Microsoft. Facebook has not yet hit the trillion dollars mark with a valuation of 0.66 trillion dollars. And now Apple is the first company to achieve a market value of two trillion dollars.

The Properties and Reversals that McLuhan Identified for Electric Media are even more Appropriate and more the Case for the Description of Digital Media

The way McLuhan characterized electric media and their reversals in Chapter Two applies with even greater validity with digital media. McLuhan characterization of the Global Village as a place where we "live in the utmost proximity" is even more the case because of the increased proximity created by our digital media of the Internet, the Web, smartphones and all of the channels that they make possible such as email, texting, Twitter, Skype, blogs and social media like Facebook and Instagram.

Knowledge and information flow unimpeded across national borders creating communities of interest and practice on a global level through the use of the Internet and the World Wide Web. The printing press gave rise to nation states and nationalism among groups of population with a common language. The Internet, on the other hand, is creating a world community, the Global Village, as McLuhan suggested. Like any village the interactions on the Internet provide both service (such as increased access to information and collaboration) and disservice (such as fake news, trolling and hate messaging). The Internet for example gives rise to an increase in populism on both the left and the right creating both service and disservice depending on your political preferences.

McLuhan identified information overload with electric media in 1967 on the CBC The Best of Ideas radio show: "One of the effects of living with electric information is that we live habitually in a state of information overload. There's always more than you can cope with." With digital media we see that information overload has increased by an order of magnitude. McLuhan observed "in the Electric Age, the amount of information available to man about himself and about the rest of mankind and about the world we live in – the amount of information available instantly and totally at all times is beyond anything that previous ages ever knew (http://inspiredangela.wordpress.com/2013/05/06/our-lady-of-good-studies-marshall-mcluhans-favorite-title-of-bvm/)." The amount of information available today compared with that available 50 years ago when the only digital devices were main frame and mini computers has increased by several orders of magnitude but still McLuhan's observations for electric media hold and are even more the case in the digital age. Other digital age properties and reversals that we will now consider include decentralization, monopolies of knowledge, consumers reverse into producers, do it yourself culture, products reverse into services, knowledge as the principal activities of humankind, interdisciplinarity, jobs reverse into roles and increased orality.

Decentralization

McLuhan observed that electric information decentralizes but with digital media such as smart phones and the Internet this is even more the case as one can be in touch with almost anyone in the world as long as they are within convenient distance of Wi-Fi or a cellular tower. The users of the Internet, no matter where they are located, find themselves at the center of a vast network of information and activity. Mobile devices even allow users to access the Internet while they are on the move. A large metropolitan city is no more at the center of the action than any smart phone or personal computer user almost anywhere on the planet.

With the industrial revolution, workers were forced to gather around big cities where factories and resources were available, but with the development of personal computers and the Internet today's information workers don't have to work at a centralized location anymore. Web servers with file sharing capabilities and Web conference software enable people to work on the road or from home, to have meetings and to pull up documents from anywhere they happened to be (https://www.coursehero.com/file/pbbur1l/QUESTION-How-has-the-development-of-personal-computer-hardware-and-software/). As a result of this there is a much greater degree of decentralization in the digital age compared with the electric age of mass media. During the Covid-19 pandemic, raging as I write these words, millions of workers were able to carry on with their jobs working from home.

The Internet, created in the middle of the Cold War to avoid a collapse of the U.S. communication network in case of a nuclear attack, operates on the principle of total decentralization. Who could have predicted then that Arpanet, the forerunner of the Internet would evolve into today's Internet that is having such a profound effect on us economically, socially, politically and culturally? This development illustrates the point that an emergent phenomenon cannot be predicted ahead of time. The fact that McLuhan was able to sketch out in very rough terms the broad outline of the Internet phenomenon even before Arpanet was created does not contradict the non-predictability of emergent phenomena. McLuhan did not predict when, where or how the Internet would emerge. He only described why the Internet would emerge. To say that a devastating tornado will strike Kansas in the next 10 years is not a really the kind of prediction that contradicts the unpredictability of an emergent phenomenon unless one can predict what town will be hit and on what date. In other words, McLuhan's predictions were qualitative, not quantitative.

Reversal of the Monopolies of Knowledge

Harold Innis defined the notion of a monopoly of knowledge where access to knowledge is restricted to a special class of knowledge workers. In the oral era it was through rhetoric or the ability to use spoken language persuasively. In the literate age before universal education those that possessed the skills of literacy were able to dominate those that were illiterate. This was the case in Babylon and ancient Egypt where monopolies of knowledge were formed by the priestly bureaucracies of scribes. The same phenomena occurred in the ancient Greek and Roman world with secret learning societies. During the Middle Ages, "monopolies of knowledge controlled by monasteries were followed by monopolies of knowledge controlled by copyist guilds in the large cities" (Innis 1951, 53).

With the emergence of the printing press these monopolies of knowledge began to break up. "Freedom of the press has been regarded as a great bulwark of our civilization and it would be dangerous to say that it has become the great bulwark of monopolies of the press" (Innis 1951, 139). But as A. J. Liebling (1960) pointed out, "**freedom of the press is guaranteed only to those who own one.**" Those that possessed or controlled a printing press could dominate their society as was the case when the dominance of the Hearst newspaper chain was able to set the agenda for the foreign policy of the USA.

Innis (1951, 129) also pointed out that science even though it embraces openness has its own form of a monopoly of knowledge, "even science with its emphasis on a common vernacular and on translations has come under the influence of monopolies of knowledge in patents, secret processes and military security measures."

Another loosening of the monopolies of knowledge occurred with electrically configured information because of the general trend with electricity to speed up the flow of information and decentralize its sources.

> Mechanization has emphasized complexity and confusion; it has been responsible for monopolies in the field of knowledge; and it becomes extremely important to any civilization, if it is not to succumb to the influence of this monopoly of knowledge, to make some critical survey and report. The conditions of the freedom of thought are in danger of being destroyed by science, technology, and the mechanization of knowledge, and with them, Western civilization (Innis 1951, 32).

The Internet and the digital revolution have furthered the breakdown of traditional monopolies of knowledge. With the Internet monopolies of knowledge have been reversing into crowd sourcing. Because of the Internet.

> the fears that Innis expressed in 1951 have largely disappeared because the increased connectivity has led to open systems in which information is free to flow and small elites are no longer as able to control the creation of wealth. The Internet and the World Wide Web have played a prominent role in the breakdown of Industrial Era monopolies of knowledge by providing a medium whereby non-professionals have been able to share their experiences and network their knowledge. Web sites that act as electronic support groups have sprung up all over the Net providing practical suggestions for those who have to cope with a variety of different medical, psychological and social conditions. Rather than a trained professional observing the suffering of individuals second hand and passing their observations on to a third party, those with firsthand experience are advising others of how they coped with and/or survived their particular challenge. This process does not compromise the role of the trained professional but it has resulted in many cases with a more effective way of sharing tacit knowledge and certainly broken down many monopolies of knowledge (Logan 2004, 60).

The above passage that I wrote in 2000 only six years into the release of Netscape and the public use of the Internet was a bit over enthusiastic and did not consider the super monopolies of organizations such as Google, Facebook, Apple, Amazon and Microsoft, which we will deal with in due course. Nevertheless, it is true that many monopolies of knowledge have broken down with the Internet and the Web.

The power of decentralization and the breakdown of monopolies of knowledge for both an electronic communication system and a social organization is that the system is robust by virtue of its redundancy. The Internet for example provides everybody with more or less equal access to the world's knowledge publicly available on the Web. This includes:

- all the open access journals;
- preprint collections such as arXiv, bioRxiv, Academia.edu, ResearchGate.net, Social Science Research Network and the following sites where books can be accessed for free:
- Project Gutenberg,
- Internet Archive,
- Open Library,
- GoogleBooks (having scanned 30 million books Google provides free access as follows: the full book for books out of copyright and partial view of books depending on the instructions of the publisher holding the book's copyright),
- Smashwords,
- Blurb,
- Scribd,
- Wattpad (https://ebookfriendly.com/sites-where-you-can-read-books-online/ accessed April 23, 2019.).

The availability of these resources is another example of decentralization, the decentralization of knowledge and library resources.

Consumers becomes Producers

"At electric speeds the consumer becomes producer as the public becomes participant role player," according to McLuhan and Nevitt (1972, 4). This is even more the case with digital media such as Facebook, Twitter, Instagram, Flickr, YouTube, LinkedIn, and blogs, where the content of these media is created by their users. Another example is the open source movement where the production of software is shared by a number of its users. Linux is an example of this, which was created when Finland's Linus Torvalds asked others to join him in improving Unix. This development also illustrates McLuhan's suggestion that individual effort reverses into the task force (McLuhan 1971).

Do It Yourself Thrives

McLuhan also suggested that with electric media that the age of manufactured goods reverses into the age of "do it yourself." He wrote, "As technology advances, it reverses the characteristics of every situation again and again. The age of automation is going to be the age of do it yourself (McLuhan 1995, 283)." This 1957 forecast foreshadowed the 3D printer which enables its users to engage in "do it yourself" manufacturing. Many of the software packages on personal computers allow users to perform tasks on their own. Desktop publishing packages allow their users to do their own typesetting. Digital cameras allow users to process their own photos and put an end to the photographic film manufacturing and the film processing businesses. Digital still and video cameras led to do it yourself photography and film making. The software Photoshop allowed their users to do their own editing of photos and videos. PC software packages such as word processing, spread sheets and data bases allowed their users to do many data processing tasks on their own.

"Products Increasingly are Becoming Services"

This observation made by McLuhan (2005a, 101) in 1966 that manufacturing as the prime engine of the economy gives way to the service sector is even more the case with digital media. The e-book which replaces many manufactured books is an example of products becoming services. Today's largest monopolies of the digital age, Amazon, Apple, Facebook, Google and Microsoft are basically service providers. The main businesses of Facebook, Google and Microsoft are providing services although some of their subsidiaries that they acquired manufacture actual products. Amazon is a service company that provides their customers to purchase and have delivered to their homes or places of business the manufactured goods and groceries that they sell. This in addition to a number of services that they also provide such as Cloud hosting. Apple which started out as a manufacturing company is very much in the services business. We remind the reader of the list of stores, services and software apps that Apple created that were married to their hardware products: iTunes, iOS App Store, Mac App Store, Apple Music, Apple TV+, iMessage, iCloud, Safari web browser, iLife, iWork, Final Cut Pro, Logic Pro, Xcode, Apple Store, Genius Bar, Apple Care, AppePay, ApplePay Cash and Apple Card. So, even though Apple Inc. is a manufacture of a variety of hardware devices it is still very much in the service business. Apple's hardware and that of other hardware manufacturers are actually the gateway to a very large array of services.

While it is true that some products are becoming services like e-books but what is increasingly the case is that the economy in the digital age is becoming more and more a service economy than a manufacturing economy. Because of AI and robots many manufacturing jobs are being lost but the number of service sector jobs is increasing. Some of those new sector service jobs are involved in maintaining the hardware and software that service the manufacturing sector. But, other service sector jobs have nothing to do with manufacturing but rather are the creation of services for the consumption by others.

The Digital Age is the Knowledge Age

McLuhan's 1964 observation that with electric media the acquisition of knowledge is the principal activities of humankind is even more true in the digital age. He wrote:

> Under electric technology the entire business of man becomes learning and knowing. In terms of what we still consider an "economy" (the Greek word for a household), this means that all forms of employment become "paid learning," and all forms of wealth result from the movement of information. (McLuhan 1964, 58).

With today's use of the techniques of knowledge management for sharing knowledge among the stakeholders in an organization that are facilitated by the use of personal computers and the Internet, McLuhan's 1964 observation is even more the case.

The Digital Age is the Age of Interdisciplinarity

McLuhan together with Fiore saw a major change in the way information would be organized with the transition to electric information: "The alphabet and print technology fostered and encouraged a fragmenting process, a process of specialism and detachment. Electric technology fosters and encourages unification and involvement (McLuhan and Fiore 1967, 8)." This is even more the case today with digital media as information, knowledge and methodologies from different disciplines are easily accessed across the Internet. Researchers googling for information might encounter useful information from a field outside their domain of expertise. McLuhan with Leonard made a similar observation. "More swiftly than we can realize, we are moving into an era dazzlingly different. Fragmentation, specialization and sameness will be replaced by wholeness, diversity and, above all, a deep involvement (McLuhan and Leonard 1967)." McLuhan who was attacked by his specialist colleagues in academe defended his approach by attacking his attackers, "The specialist is one who never makes small mistakes while moving toward the grand fallacy (McLuhan 1964, 124)" and "the specialist is the one who stays put (https://www.mediaeducationcentre.eu/eng/?page_id=442 accessed November 16, 2019)."

In the Digital Age there is a Greater Focus on Role-Playing versus Job Holding

McLuhan's (1969a, 28) observation that "with the acceleration of information movement … the consequence of automation may well mean the end of the single job for the single lifetime" is even more the case some 50 years later in this the digital age. And it is certainly true that McLuhan's electric age observation that goal-seeking or jobs reverse into role-playing is more the case with digital media in the knowledge age. Very few people these days remain with the same company throughout their working career but rather jump from one company to another and from one position or job type within a company to another. The generalist has replaced the specialist.

Increased Reversal into Orality in the Digital Age

McLuhan noted that with electric mass media there was a return to the pattern of orality. According to him "everybody lives in the utmost proximity created by our electric involvement in one another's lives (McLuhan 1964, 35)." And living in close proximity re-creates the patterns of oral cultures. Ong described this reversal in terms of secondary orality, the orality of a culture in possession of the written word. "The electronic age is also an age of 'secondary orality,' the orality of telephones, radio, and television, which depends on writing and print for its existence (Ong 2002, 2)." Although many radio and TV shows make use of orality often that orality is scripted and hence differs from primary orality of a culture that does not possess writing. Even unscripted orality in every day conversations in a literate culture possesses structures that mimic written expression.

The reversal into orality becomes even more prominent with digital media. Access to audio and video increased with the Internet and its associated streaming. But with the Internet an oral component also crept into written expression particularly with the channels of email, Twitter and social media. With the rapidification of digital communication the users of the Internet do not have time for the niceties of proper grammar and if something can be said with an emoji all the better. The syntax or lack of syntax of these forms of written expression have an oral character to them. Although the written dialogue is visual and not aural the syntax of the written Internet-based digital text duplicates many features of the spoken word. Ong described this phenomenon as secondary literacy and alternately as tertiary orality in an interview he gave in 1996 when describing the nature of the written word in digital media:

> When I first used the term 'secondary orality,' I was thinking of the kind of orality you get on radio and television, where oral performance produces effects somewhat like those of 'primary orality,' the orality using the unprocessed human voice, particularly in addressing groups, but where the creation of orality is of a new sort. Orality here is produced by technology. Radio and television are 'secondary' in the sense that they are technologically powered, demanding the use of writing and other technologies in designing and manufacturing the machines which reproduce voice. They are thus unlike primary orality, which uses no tools or technology at all. Radio and television provide technologized orality. This is what I originally referred to by the term 'secondary orality.'
>
> I have also heard the term 'secondary orality' lately applied by some to other sorts of electronic verbalization which are really not oral at all—to the Internet and similar computerized creations for text. There is a reason for this usage of the term. In non-technologized oral interchange, as we have noted earlier, there is no perceptible interval between the utterance of the speaker and the hearer's reception of what is uttered. Oral communication is all immediate, in the present. Writing, chirographic or typed, on the other hand, comes out of the past. Even if you write a memo to yourself, when you refer to it, it's a memo which you wrote a few minutes ago, or maybe two weeks ago. But on a computer network, the recipient can receive what is communicated with no such interval. Although it is not exactly the same as oral communication, the network message from one person to another or others is very rapid and can in effect be in the present. Computerized communication can thus suggest the immediate experience of direct sound. I believe that is why computerized verbalization has been assimilated to secondary 'orality,' even when it comes not in oral-aural format but through the eye, and thus is not directly oral at all. Here textualized verbal exchange registers psychologically as having the temporal immediacy of oral exchange. To handle [page break] such technologizing of the textualized word, I have tried occasionally to introduce the term 'secondary literacy.' We are not considering here the production of sounded words on the computer, which of course are even more readily assimilated to 'secondary orality' (Kleine & Gale 1996)

More Electric Age Reversals Enhanced by Digital Media

McLuhan identified a number of reversals that took place as a result of the transition from the age of written communication to the age of electric communication. In this section we provide a list of these reversals that in each instance are enhanced or are more the case with digital based communication. Here they are in no particular order:

- pattern of electric communication reverses into pattern of oral communication;
- visual space reverses into acoustic space;
- linear causal connections reverse into a field or ecological approach;
- linear sequential mechanical ordering reverses into instantaneity and all-at-onceness;
- mainframe computers reverse into personal computers {this was a prediction McLuhan made implicitly when he told a group of IBM executive there would be a computer in every home way back in 1968 (Nevitt and McLuhan 1994, 29–30).};
- fragmentation, specialization reverses into wholeness, diversity, involvement;
- separation of function reverses into integrated and organic integration;
- detachment reverses into involvement;
- classification reverses into pattern recognition;
- fixed point of view reverses into interface and pattern;
- connection reverses into pattern;
- answers reverse into questions in education;
- hardware reverses into software;
- explosion reverses into implosion;
- local culture reverses into universal global culture;
- Eastern cultural forms reverse into Western cultural forms and Western cultural forms reverse into Eastern cultural forms.

Exploiting McLuhan's Laws of Media (LoM) to Better Understand the Technology of the Digital Age and their Associated Reversals

The reader should note that we will be considering two types of reversals:

1. the reversals that a class of media produce in the perceptual, social, economic and political aspects of society during the transition from one class of media to another; and
2. the reversal in the fourth law of the Laws of Media (LoM) in which a medium when pushed to its limits reverses or flips into a complementary medium.

The Reversals from One Age of Technology to Another

Before beginning the reversals that characterize the digital age we will first examine the transitions from the very first forms of tools, namely hand tools to the tools of the digital age. We will perform a series of LoM analyzes that describe the dynamics of the reversals from one age of technology to another. In particular we will examine the transitions from the following reversals:

- from the age of hand tools to
- the age of mechanical technologies and then the reversal to
- the age of steam powered technologies and then the reversal to
- the age of petroleum powered technologies and then the reversal to
- the age of electric tools and media and then the reversal to
- the age of digital technologies.

We will discover through the use of the LoM analyzes that each of the ages we are considering basically entail a reversal from the previous age followed by a reversal into the next age: namely hand tools reverse into mechanical technology which then reverse into steam powered tools. Steam powered tools reverse into both petroleum powered machines and electric powered tools. And electric powered tools then reverse into electric media which then reverse into digital media.

Hand tools:
Enhance: muscle power and extend the human body (the first hand tools appeared before the arrival of humans starting with Australopithecus 3.4 million years ago by and then by various members of genus Homo including finally modern humans).
Obsolesce: non-hominids.
Retrieve: the hand and the opposable thumb.
Reverse: into mechanical technologies (3000 BC for draught animals; 400 BC for water wheels and 500 AD for wind power).

Mechanical technology:
Enhances: animal, water and wind power for use in agriculture, mass production manufacturing and food processing.
Obsolesces: handcraft and hand tools.
Retrieves: the horn of plenty.
Reverses: into the steam engine (1712 for Newcomen steam engine) and steam-powered technology (1775 for the Watt steam engine that incorporates rotary motion).

Steam powered tools:
Enhance: manufacture and transportation (steam ships and locomotives).
Obsolesce: the water wheel, the windmill and animal power.
Retrieve: slave labor.
Reverse: into electric power (1882) and petroleum power (1885).

Petroleum powered machines:
Enhance: transportation through the automobile and other types of motorized vehicles.
Obsolesce: the horse and buggy.
Retrieve: the knight in shining armour with their shiny new automobile (McLuhan, M. & E. McLuhan 1988, 148).
Reverse: into pollution and traffic jams.

Electric powered tools:
Enhance: machines.
Obsolesce: steam power.
Retrieve: the servant (in terms of household appliances like the washing machine and the vacuum cleaner).
Reverse: into robots, hybrid technologies, electric media.

Electric media:
Enhance: mass communication.
Obsolesce: the printing press.
Retrieve: oral culture.
Reverse: into interactive digital media.

Digital "new media":
Enhance: interactivity, access to information, and two-way communication.
Obsolesce: mass media.
Retrieve: community.
Reverse: into hybrid media.

Reversals with Hybrid or Convergent Technologies

Next, we do a LoM and reversal analysis for the class of hybrid technologies since the one characteristics of all digital age media is that they are all complex hybrid technologies. All technologies are hybrids in the sense that they combine simpler components. The hatchet with a handle is a simple hybrid technology consisting of a hand axe and a lever (the handle). Digital media, on the other hand, are complex hybrid technologies in two senses. Like all technologies they are composed of simpler components, but what is unique about digital media is that they combine and hybridize functions to a much greater extent that nondigital media. Digital media being hybrids create new functionalities and release new forms of energy, as McLuhan (1964, 48) suggested more than fifty years ago, when he wrote, "The crossing or hybridization of the media release great new forces and energy by fission and fusion." The second factor that differentiates digital hybrid technologies from non-digital hybrid technologies is that digital hybrid technologies are also interconnected with each other through the Internet and the Web.

Hybrid technologies:
Enhance: convenience.
Obsolesce: the clutter of many individual devices.
Retrieve: the Swiss Army knife or the even older Delphian knife as described by Aristotle.
Reverse: into interconnected hybrid technologies with a higher level of complexity (for example a stand-alone PC reverses into a PC connected to the Internet and the World Wide Web).

Digital Age Reversals Beginning with the Introduction of Personal Computers

We are now ready turn to the LoMs and reversals from the electric age technologies to The various devices and artifacts introduced in the digital age beginning with the personal computer, which as has been suggested kicked off the digital age.

In this section we will look at the following developments that characterize what we have termed the Digital Age: personal computers (desktops, laptops and notebooks which perform the same functions and only differ in their size increasing their mobility); tablets; word processing; desktop publishing; the multifunction printer; the scanner and OCR software; the Internet; Wi-Fi; email; Internet Browsers, the World Wide Web; search engines; the Cloud; social media; Facebook; Instagram; Snapchat; Twitter; blogs; podcasts; YouTube and Vimeo; e-books; Reddit; Tinder; Skype; the smartphone; AI; and robots.

Personal computers (or PCs including desktop, laptop, and notebook versions):
Enhance: access to computing (amplifies speed of calculations and the retrieval of information).
Obsolesce: many applications of mainframe and mini computers that the PC can now execute; also obsolesces need to do computing in a highly centralized location.
Retrieve: the personal assistant;

Reverse: into the tablet computer.

- Main frame and mini computers reverse into various forms of personal computing including desktop, laptop, and notebook computers.

Tablet computers:
Enhance: mobile access to computing and information retrieval with a touch screen interface.
Obsolesce: personal computers.
Retrieve: the personal assistant who accompanies the users wherever they go.
Reverse: into even greater information overload.

- Personal computers reverse into tablet computers.

Word Processing:
Enhances: written composition.
Obsolesces: hand writing.
Retrieves: the scribe dedicated to producing the written word.
Reverses: into desktop publishing.

- Hand writing with pen and paper reverses into word processing.

Desktop Publishing:
Enhances: typesetting.
Obsolesces: lead fonts and mechanical typesetting.
Retrieves: Gutenberg.
Reverses: into self-publishing.

- Commercial publishers reverse into every person a publisher, that is, self-publishing with the Internet.

The Multifunction Printer:
Enhances: the distribution and reproduction of the written word and graphic images and hence extends the eye.
Obsolesces: mimeograph and carbon paper.
Retrieves: sharing of visual information (in a written or graphic form) but in the manner of oral society; that is, visual material shared acoustically.
Reverse: into "everybody becomes a publisher" (McLuhan, M. and McLuhan, E. 1988, 145).

- Photocopying reverses into the multifunction printer.

The Scanner and OCR Software:
Enhances: reproduction, digitization, and distribution of text documents and images.
Obsolesces: the photocopier.
Retrieves: the copyist or scribe.
Reverses: into document glut.

- Photocopying reverses into the scanner and OCR software.

The Internet:
Enhances: connectivity to information resources and to other computer users.
Obsolesces: teletype and fax as well as the specialist and/or library as the exclusive sources of information.
Retrieves: community but non-locally in the form of a Global Village.
Reverses: into information overload, masquerade, spamming, scamming and hacking.

- International telecommunications and local area networks (LANs) reverse into the Internet.

Email:
Enhances: interpersonal connections and group communication.
Obsolesces: telephone calls.
Retrieves: letter writing, the newsletter and the town crier.
Reverses: into spam (junk email); scams.

- Phone calls, letter writing and post cards reverse into email.

The World Wide Web:
Enhances: two-way communication, access to information, and continuous learning.
Obsolesces: newspapers, magazines, academic print journals, and paper-based communication in general.
Retrieves: alignment and community.
Reverses: into a platform for games, music, audios, photos, and videos, as well as a platform for a number of negative activities such as cyberbullying, hate messaging, the recruitment of terrorists, harmful forms of hacking such as identity theft and misuse of personal data.

- Usenet and Bulletin Boards reverse into the World Wide Web.

Search Engines:
Enhance: rapid location and retrieval of Web-based information.
Obsolesce: catalogues such as library card catalogues.
Retrieve: the paper-based index and table of contents.
Reverse: into the online index and table of contents of the ever-expanding document that is the content of the Web.

- Library card catalogues and catalogues in general reverse into Google and other search engines.

The Cloud:
Enhances: storage of large amounts of data.
Obsolesces: the external drives of computers.
Retrieves: the Library at Alexandria.
Reverses: into information glut.

- Networked mainframe computers acting as servers reverse into the Cloud.

Social Media:
Enhance: online connections and non-local friendships; the image of the user of social media site.
Obsolesce: face-to-face socialization and real life.
Retrieve: long distance correspondence; Narcissus and masquerade.
Reverses: into social isolation; online virtual life and socializing; and fake identities.

- Face-to-face socializing reverses into social media interactions.

Facebook:
Enhances: making and maintaining online acquaintanceships and friendships.
Obsolesces: meaningful friendships.
Retrieves: popularity as the criteria of social success.
Flips: into loneliness; a substitute for real experiences; misuse of users' personal information as occurred when Cambridge Analytica used personal data to influence Trump's 2016 presidential election and the Brexit referendum.

- The Web reverses into social media like Facebook.

Instagram:
Enhances: sharing photos and videos; vanity; self-esteem; visual representation; taking photos and creating videos; online social interactions; flirting.

Obsolesces: text; physical photographs.
Retrieves: Narcissus; past experiences and adventures; the photo album.
Reverses into: imagery versus substance; opportunity for notoriety; beauty competition; envy.

- Facebook reverses into Instagram.

SnapChat:
Enhances: visual dimension of online conversations; shock value; self-esteem; opportunities for humor; rapid communication; selfie culture; flirting.
Obsolesces: a record of the communication; video chats.
Retrieves: flashing; practical jokes.
Flips or Reverses into: sexting; vapid interactions; vulgarity.

- Instagram reverses into SnapChat.

Twitter:
Enhances: immediate online communication to multiple followers.
Obsolesces: email; breaking-news bulletins on TV; newspaper headlines.
Retrieves: the telegram and telex, PR.
Reverses: into narcissism and the banal; unsubstantiated claims; fake news.

- Telegrams, news bulletins and email reverse into tweets.

Blogs:
Enhance: publishing, the exchange of information between bloggers and their readers.
Obsolesce: newsletters, physical bulletin boards, and communications sent through the postal system.
Retrieve: communities of interest.
Reverse: into self-promotion.

- Newspaper columns and newsletters reverse into blogs.

Podcasts:
Enhance: oral communication and visual communication in the case of visual podcasts or vlogs.
Obsolesce: live lectures and oral presentations.
Retrieve: alignment and community; radio talk shows.

Reverse: into competition with commercial radio.

- Radio talk shows and lectures reverse into podcasts.

YouTube, Vimeo:
Enhances: access to and sharing of audio and video files.
Obsolesces: real time commercial television.
Retrieves: vintage movies, radio shows, recordings and television shows.
Reverses: into an audio and visual archive of past performances and events.

- Television and radio shows, films, audio recordings reverse into YouTube and Vimeo.

e-books:
Enhance: the accessibility of a book.
Obsolesce: the printed codex book.
Retrieve: the convenience of the original pocket-size paperback book.
Reverse: into self-publishing and print on demand.

- Print books reverse into e-books.

Reddit:
Enhances: exchange of social news.
Obsolesces: newsletters and newspapers.
Retrieves: gossip.
Reverses: into a network of communities.

- Social group newsletters reverse into Reddit.

Tinder and other online dating sites:
Enhance: self-introductions; pick-ups; dating; self-esteem; flirting; social life.
Obsolesce: pick-up bars, blind dates; traditional dating; introductions by friends; fix-ups.
Retrieve: one-night stands; promiscuity; casual dating.
Reverse: into hook-ups, but occasionally into long-term relationships including marriage.

- Pick-ups at bars and fix-ups reverse into online dating apps.

Skype, Zoom and other VoIPs (voice over IP):
Enhance: long distance communication with a visual component; low cost communication of data; long distant relationships.
Obsolesce: long distance telephoning and faxing; in person interviews; travel for meetings.
Retrieve: face-to-face meetings; telex; fax.
Reverse: into Web/video conferencing; VoIP spam or SPIT (spam over Internet telephony).

- Long distance phone calls and faxes reverse into Skype.

The Smartphone:
Enhances: the mobile access to information as the Swiss Army knife or the handyman's tool box of telecommunications.
Obsolesces: the cell phone, the land line, access to Wi-Fi.
Retrieves: the Internet and/or friends at any time and any place as well as the personal assistant who accompanies the users wherever they go.
Reverses: into an obsession with the present moment and loss of touch with reality.

- Landline telephone reverses into cell phones which then reverse into smartphones ["With telephone and TV it is not so much the message as the sender that is 'sent' (McLuhan and Nevitt 1972, 223)."].

Artificial Intelligence (AI):
Enhances: decision making by algorithm.
Obsolesces: human decision making in certain domains.
Retrieves: a consultant and/or an assistant.
Reverses: into the idea of the Singularity and the devaluing of the notion of what constitutes human intelligence.

- Automation reverses into AI ["Computers can do better than ever what needn't be done at all. Making sense is still a human monopoly." (McLuhan and Nevitt 1972, 109)].

Robots:
Enhance: automation.
Obsolesce: human labour.
Retrieve: slaves.

Reverse: into dehumanization of the work place.

- Automation reverses into robotics.

Other Digital Age Reversals
In addition to the digital age reversals that McLuhan identified through his analysis of electric age media or the reversals we identified using his Laws of Media there are some other reversal worthy of notice. Perhaps the most significant reversal is the loss of privacy that the use of Internet based digital media entails. This is such a large topic we address it in the chapter following this one, Understanding Humans: The Extensions of Digital Media.

Another reversal worth noting is the one from couch potatoes to digital zombies. During the age of electric media viewers spent an inordinate amount of time in the front of their television sets that came to be known as "boob tubes" or the "idiot boxes." Television watching particularly among the digital generation has been replaced by smartphone and tablet watching producing what I will call digital zombies. This is not my coinage. There is, in fact, a Wikipedia article on digital zombies which defines a digital zombie as "a person so engaged with digital technology they are unable to separate themselves from a persistent online presence (https://en.wikipedia.org/wiki/Digital_Zombie, accessed November 17, 2019)." According to Reader's Digest (https://www.rd.com/culture/texting-and-walking-injuries, accessed November 17, 2019) there have been multiple injuries to digital zombies crossing the road while focused on their smartphone about a 1000 injuries per year. Many municipalities have instituted fines for people engaged in distracted walking.

Smartphone addictions is a new digital age phenomenon as the following statistics reveal:

- 92% of Americans believe smartphone addiction is real.
- 43% of millennials check their phone at least every 20 minutes.
- 60% think they touch their phones 100 times or less per day a typical user taps, touches or swipes their phone 2617 times per day.
- 20% check their phone every 20 minutes; 14% every 30 minutes; 25% every hour; 19% every 2–3 hours; 10% every 3–5 hours; 10% about twice a day; and 2% never put it down.
- 70% say it's inappropriate to have a smartphone out during a meeting; but 53% do it anyway.
- 80% say it's inappropriate to check their phone during a meeting; but 50% do it anyway.

- 10% have had their phone out during an interview.
- 77% bring their phone into the bathroom at work. (www.socialmediatoday/news/smartphone-etiquette-2018-infographic/531993, accessed September 13, 2019).

References

Innis, Harold. *The Bias of Communication*. Toronto: University of Toronto Press, 1951.

Kleine, Michael, and Fredric G. Gale. "The Elusive Presence of the Word: An Interview with Walter Ong." *Composition FORUM* 7.2 (Fall 1996): 65–86.

Liebling, A. J. "The Wayward Press: Do You Belong in Journalism?" *New Yorker* (May 14, 1960): 109.

Logan, Robert K. *The Sixth Language: Learning a Living in the Internet Age*. Caldwell, NJ: Blackburn Press (1st edition 2000. Toronto: Stoddart Publishing; Mandarin Edition ISBN 986-7964-05-5), 2004.

McLuhan, Marshall. *Understanding Media: Extensions of Man*. New York: McGraw Hill. (The page references in the text are for the McGraw Hill paperback second edition. Readers should be aware that the pagination in other editions is different.), 1964.

McLuhan, Marshall. "Playboy Magazine Interview." *Playboy* 16, no. 3 (March, 1969): 53–74, 158.

McLuhan, Marshall. *Culture Is Our Business*. New York and Toronto: McGraw-Hill, 1970.

McLuhan, Marshall. "Marshall McLuhan Convocation Address, The University of Alberta", 1971. http://projects.chass.utoronto.ca/mcluhan-studies/v1_iss5/1_5art3.htm. Accessed April 16, 2019.

McLuhan, Marshall. "At the Moment of Sputnik the Planet became a Global Theater in which There are No Spectators but Only Actors." *Journal of Communication* 24, no. 1 (1974): 48–58.

McLuhan, Marshall. "II. Media Evolution, Media Forms, Language and Speech." In *Essential McLuhan*, edited by Eric McLuhan and Frank Zingrone. Concord, ON: Anansi, 1995.

McLuhan, Marshall. "The Relation of Environment to Anti-Environment." In *Media Research: Technology, Art and Communication*, edited by Michael Moos, 110–20. Abington, UK: Routledge, 1997.

McLuhan, Marshall. "Predicting Communication Via the Internet." In *Understanding Me: Lectures and Interviews*, edited by Stephanie McLuhan and David Staines. Cambridge, MA: MIT Press, 2005.

McLuhan, Marshall, and Quentin Fiore. *The Medium is the Massage: An Inventory of Effects*. New York: Random House, 1967.

McLuhan, Marshall, and George B. Leonard. "The Future of Education: The Class of 1989." *Look Magazine* (Feb 21, 1967): 23–25.

McLuhan, Marshall, and Barrington Nevitt. *Take Today: The Executive as Dropout*. Toronto: Longman Canada, 1972.

McLuhan, Marshall, and Eric McLuhan. *Laws of Media: The New Science*. Toronto: University of Toronto Press, 1988.

Nevitt, Barrington, and Maurice McLuhan. *Who Was Marshall McLuhan?* Toronto: Stoddart Publishing, 1994.

Ong, Walter. *Orality and Literacy: The Technologizing of the Word* (2nd ed.). New York: Routledge, 2002.

CHAPTER FOUR

Understanding Humans: The Extensions of Digital Media

Technologies are merely extensions of ourselves – McLuhan (1967a, 261)

All media are extensions of some human faculty — psychic or physical – McLuhan & Fiore (1967)

Digital industrialism turns human data into the new commodity - Rushkoff (2016, 44)

This is Google's model of giving away everything in return for looking at their ads and sharing all our data - Rushkoff (ibid., 37)

Introduction

The idea that our tools are extensions of our body is an idea that dates back to the latter half of the nineteenth century. Ralph Waldo Emerson (1875) in 1870 wrote: "All the tools and engines on earth are only extensions of man's limbs and senses." And Henry Ward Beecher in 1887 wrote, "A tool is but the extension of a man's hand and a machine is but a complex tool." This idea was then picked up by C. K. Ogden and I. A. Richards (1923, 98) in their book, *The Meaning of Meaning*, where they wrote: "But language, though often spoken of as a medium of communication is best regarded as an instrument; and all instruments are extensions or refinements of our sense organs." Lewis Mumford (1934, 321) also dealt with this theme in *Technics and Civilization*:

> The tools and utensils used during the greater part of man's history were, in the main, extensions of his own organism; they did not seem to have-what is more important they did not seem to have-an independent existence. But though they were an intimate part of the worker, they reacted upon his capacities, sharpening his eyes, refining his skill, teaching him to respect the nature of the material with which he was dealing. The tool brought man into closer harmony with his environment, not merely because it enabled him to re-shape it, but because it made him recognize the limits of his capacities. In dream, he was all powerful: in reality he had to recognize the weight of stone and cut stones no bigger than he could transport.

McLuhan who was familiar with both Ogden and Richards paper and Mumford's book made use of this idea in his book *Understanding Media: The Extensions of Man* (McLuhan 1964) where it became a central theme of his understanding of media and technology and their effects. McLuhan wrote:

> This is merely to say that the personal and social consequences of any medium-- that is, of any **extension of ourselves** -- result from the new scale that is introduced into our affairs by each **extension of ourselves**, or by any new technology …

> Physiologically, man (sic) in the normal use of technology (**or his variously extended body**) is perpetually modified by it and in turn finds ever new ways of modifying his technology. Man (sic) becomes, as it were, the sex organs of the machine world, as the bee of the plant world, enabling it to fecundate and to evolve ever new forms. The machine world reciprocates man's (sic) love by expediting his wishes and desires, namely, in providing him with wealth (McLuhan 1964, 23; 55–56; bolding is mine).

McLuhan made use of the theme of media as "extensions of man" throughout his career. He wrote with Quentin Fiore in *The Medium is The Massage: An Inventory of Effects*: "All media are extensions of some human faculty – psychic or physical (McLuhan and Fiore 1967, 26)." With Barrington Nevitt in *Take Today: Executive as Dropout* he wrote, "Environments work us over and remake us. It is man who is the *content* of and the *message* of the *media*, which are extensions of himself (McLuhan and Nevitt 1972, 90)."

McLuhan's notion of media as "extensions of man" which he formulated before the digital age also holds true for today's technologies. His insights into electric media apply with equal validity for many of the features of digital technology. He seems to have foreshadowed the Internet, Wikipedia, and Google when he wrote: "A computer as a research and communication instrument could enhance retrieval, obsolesce mass library organization, retrieve individual encyclopedic function and flip into a private line to speedily tailored data of a saleable kind (McLuhan 1995, 295–96)."

The sense in which the data provided by companies like Google is of a "saleable kind" is that Google and other search engine companies receive revenue from advertisers for the advertisements that accompany the data that we request from Google or other search engine companies.

McLuhan developed the Laws of Media as a technique for analyzing media. It consists of four laws, namely, that every medium, tool or human artifact enhances some human function (Law 1); obsolesces a former way of achieving that function (Law 2); retrieves something from the past that has been obsolesced (Law 3); and according to Law 4 any technology pushed far enough **flips or reverses** into its opposite or complementary form.

Applying the Laws of Media to digital media we find that:

> Digital new media **enhance** interactivity, access to information, and two-way communication.
>
> They **obsolesce** mass media, like television and newspapers.
>
> They **retrieve** community, albeit an online one.
>
> And pushed far enough they **flip or reverse** into hyperreality or the loss of contact with nature and our bodies.

I believe there is another flip or reversal associated with digital media, namely the reversal of the notion that media are extensions of man. McLuhan suggested that human communications could be divided into the eras of oral, written and electric communication. Despite not having experienced the digital age which began with the emergence of the personal computer, the Internet and the Web, McLuhan seems to have anticipated many of the features of the digital era. Because digital technology pushes electric technology to its extreme it causes a flip or a reversal of the effects of this class of technologies. The flip is that not only are digital media an extension of the psyche of the user as is the case with oral, written and electric media, but it is also the case that the user actually becomes an extension of his digital technology unlike the situation in the earlier ages of non-digital media.

Culkin (1967) wrote that "we shape our tools and thereafter they shape us." Culkin's formulation is basically a reformulation of McLuhan's remark that the users of technology "is perpetually modified by it, [their technology]." With digital media there is the added feature that the use of the digital media that we humans shaped is reshaped through our use of those media by the data we enter into them.

Let us explain the sense in which I believe that users become the extensions of their digital media. In addition to the hardware and software of which digital media systems are composed they are also composed by the data that is stored within them, that is, the Big Data that sits on their servers. Most of that data or information comes directly from the users of the system as every key stroke and choice they make is information that is fed into that Big Data system as Rushkoff (2016, 90–91) explained in *Throwing Rocks at the Google Bus*:

> Projects such as IBM's Watson or Google's Machine Learning lab are not augmenting human intelligence so much as creating systems that think for themselves. With every keystroke and mouse click we make; their algorithms learn more about us while simultaneously becoming more complex than we—or anyone — can comprehend. They are getting smarter while we humans are getting relatively, or perhaps absolutely, dumber. Our machines slowly learn how to manipulate us. It's a field now called captology: the study of how computers and interfaces can influence human behavior.

The data associated with the reactions to the "speedily tailored data of a saleable kind (McLuhan 1995, 295–96)," with which the users of the information system are provided, unbeknownst to them, is captured and literally become an extension of that information system. The users of a digital information system literally become an extension of that technology, that is, de facto the content of the medium with which they are interacting. So, we have a reciprocal relationship between the human user and the digital information system. They are each an extension of each other, the information system an extension of the user and the user an extension of the information system.

This content, the human user's data as the content of the information system they are interacting with, is different than the 'content' McLuhan referred to in his one liner "the user is the content." The content in "the user is the content" is the way the users of an information system interpret the data they encounter. With digital media, the system itself is also interpreting. It is interpreting the user's data that literally become part of the content of that information system as the user's keystrokes and the data those keystrokes represent are incorporated into the Big Data that comprises the information system. This way we become an extension of that digital medium and it somehow seems to fulfill a sentiment McLuhan (1964, 64) prophesized when he wrote: "In this electronic age we see ourselves being translated more and more into the form of information, moving toward the technological extension of consciousness."

The digital media being an extension of us and at the same time we becoming an extension of our digital media is a cybernetic feedback loop in which we become trapped and at the mercy of the creators and controllers of the digital information systems with which we interact. It has always been the case that a medium or tool had a certain control over us as a user of that medium or tool as described by McLuhan and Fiore (1967, 26): "All media work us over completely. They are so persuasive in their personal, political, economic, aesthetic, psychological, moral, ethical, and social consequences that they leave no part of us untouched, unaffected, unaltered. The medium is the massage."

But the control of digital media is even more insidious because it is an invasion of our privacy and it is about us personally as we become "an item in a data bank." "Electronic man wears his brain outside his skull and his nervous system on top of his skin. He is like an exposed spider squatting in a thrumming web. But he is not flesh and blood; he is an item in a data bank, ephemeral, easily forgotten, and resentful of that fact (McLuhan and Powers 1989, 94)." This is yet another successful McLuhan prediction and it is also what McLuhan (1969a) meant when he wrote, "The more the data banks record about each one of us, the less we exist."

The Danger of Digital Monopolies

As extensions of our digital technology the problem that arises is because of the monopolies that digital media creates such as Google, Facebook, Instagram, Amazon, Yahoo, Twitter, Apple and Microsoft. The potential for their abuse is great. When our technologies were only extensions of us they enhanced our capabilities and we were in command of them in the sense that they did our bidding as their servomechanisms. The tools no doubt affected us but they were not used by others to control us. That is no longer the case with digital media because those that control digital information systems can use the data we key into their systems to manipulate us. The field of captology has the direct aim of manipulating our behavior by make use of what they learn about us. We have always been manipulated by media through advertising with newspapers, magazines, radio, and television but not to the same degree as is the case with digital media and as is the case with search engines and social media.

Captology

Captology was started by BJ Fogg (http://captology.stanford.edu/resources/thoughts-on-persuasive-technology.html) who describes captology in the following terms.

> After we ran a number of experiments, and after these studies were replicated elsewhere, the results were undeniable. Computers could indeed be designed to influence people, to change their thoughts and behaviors … Today, we are surrounded by persuasive technologies. Everywhere that digital media touches our lives, more and more there is an element of persuasion; a design created by humans and implemented in code to influence what we think, and more and more, what we do. We are surrounded. Persuasive technology is in our living rooms, in our cars. When we communicate with our loved ones online, through Facebook, persuasion is there. When we withdraw

money from the bank at the ATM, an element of persuasion may be there. When we purchase a gift online for a birthday, once again, we are being exposed to persuasion. In fact, we carry a persuasive platform, the mobile phone, with us most everywhere we go.

The Internet gives us the illusion of being part of a two-way channel of communication. The reality and the danger are that we are becoming extensions of our digital technologies controlled by the monopolies of the Internet that dominate this medium of media. We are not suggesting that any of the organizations that we listed above have any malicious intents, they just want to make money, as much as is possible, but still when the concentration of computing power becomes so great the possibility of malevolent actions is something we need to think about. There is always a danger when control of the dominant technology of a culture is in the hands of a small number of agents.

Many years before digital media invaded our world McLuhan (1964, 73) warned against this invasion of our privacy when he wrote,

> Once we have surrendered our senses and nervous systems to the private manipulation of those who would try to benefit from taking a lease on our eyes and ears and nerves, we don't really have any rights left. Leasing our eyes and ears and nerves to commercial interests is like handing over the common speech to a private corporation, or like giving the earth's atmosphere to a company as a monopoly.

More Reversals with Digital Media

There is another flip with digital media in addition to the reversal where the users become the extension of their media. Our tools or media comprise the environment or ground in which we operate. That is still true with digital media but we as the users of digital media become the ground in which digital media operate as their effectiveness depends on the information ground that we, their users create and provide them inadvertently. So, we have the flip of digital media operating in the information ground of their users in addition to their users operating in the ground of the very same digital media. The feedback of the users become the feedforward for the digital media.

There is even the reversal of McLuhan's signature one-liner "the medium is the message" which reverses into "the user is the message." The user's information becomes the content of the digital medium. That data is then tailored to exploit the needs, interests and desires of the user to the advantage of the operators or owners of the digital medium and the clients of that digital medium, who use the data they collect from the visitors to their sites for their commercial interests. Not only are the effects of digital media subliminal like all other media but the appropriation of the user's data is also subliminal in that the user is unaware of the process. In addition to the visitor to an Internet site becoming a user of the site the site becomes a user of the visitor. Just as there is no privacy in a village it is also the case that there is no privacy in the global village of the Internet. Finally, there is a new reversal of cause and effect in that the effect of users using a Web site becomes the cause of the Web site using the visitors' data and eventually the users. This development represents a new monopoly of knowledge of those that control the information systems that harvest their users' information. In a certain sense they have more information about us their users than we, the users, have about ourselves.

Conclusion

Digital technology and specifically the Internet and the Web seemed to hold the promise of the liberation of the 99% from the 1% that control the wealth of the planet and its channels of communication. It looked like freedom of the press was not going to belong only to those that owned one but with two-way flow of information finally the 99%-ers could find a voice. This has certainly happened to a certain degree. What we did not see was that the two-way flow of information not only allows for self-expression for all (at least for those with access to the Net) but it also allows the large monopolies that dominate the Internet to exploit without our permission the information and data we generate unintentionally while visiting their sites.

References

Beecher, Henry Ward. *Proverbs from Plymouth Pulpit*. Berlin: Theclassics.us, 1887.
Culkin, John. "A Schoolman's Guide to Marshall McLuhan." *Saturday Review* 51–53 (March 18, 1967): 71–72.
Emerson, Ralph Waldo. *Society and Solitude: Twelve Chapters*. Boston: James R. Osgood and Company, 1875.
McLuhan, Marshall. *Understanding Media: Extensions of Man*. New York: McGraw Hill, 1964. (The page references in the text are for the McGraw Hill paperback second edition. Readers should be aware that the pagination in other editions is different.)
McLuhan, Marshall. "Casting my Perils before Swains." In *McLuhan Hot and Cool*, edited by Gerard Emanuel Stearn. New York: Dial Press, 1967.
McLuhan, Marshall. "Computer." In *Essential McLuhan*, edited by Eric McLuhan and Frank Zingrone. Concord, ON: Anansi, 1995.

McLuhan, Marshall, and Quentin Fiore. *The Medium is the Massage: An Inventory of Effects.* New York: Random House, 1967.

McLuhan, Marshall, and Barrington Nevitt. *Take Today: The Executive as Dropout.* Toronto: Longman Canada, 1972.

McLuhan, Marshall, and Bruce R. Powers. *The Global Village: Transformations in World Life and Media in the 21st Century.* New York: Oxford University Press, 1989.

Mumford, Lewis. *Technics and Civilization.* London: Routledge and Kegan Paul, 1934.

Ogden, Charles Kay, and Ivor Armstrong Richards. *The Meaning of Meaning.* New York: Harcourt, Brace & World, 1923.

Rushkoff, Douglas. *Throwing Rocks at the Google Bus.* New York: Portfolio, 2016.

CHAPTER FIVE

General System Thinking and Marshall McLuhan's General Theory of Media

Introduction

The hardest part of scholarship is asking a pertinent question and the easier part is answering that question. I want to thank Philip Morais for asking the question "What is the most important thing that Marshall McLuhan contributed?" This chapter is my attempt to answer that question. When Phillip asked me this question during a phone conversation on the evening of January 10, 2020 my off the cuff answer was "the most important thing that Marshall McLuhan contributed was the application of general systems thinking to the study of communications and the impact of technology." I should mention that before Philip called me I had already written the first four chapters of this book and what is now Chapter Six. But as a result of Philip's question I realized that my book was incomplete and as a result I answered his question as best I could. And the answer is that the most important thing that Marshall McLuhan contributed to our understanding of media and technology and their effects is his application of general systems thinking to media studies and what came to be known as media ecology.

In Chapter One, I mentioned the influence on McLuhan of seven systems thinkers: Gregory Bateson, Ludwig von Bertalanffy, Kenneth Boulding, Buckminster Fuller, Harold Innis, I. A. Richards, Claude Shannon and Norbert Wiener. The books of these eight systems thinkers were on McLuhan's reading lists for the courses he taught. Donald Theall (2001, 30, 188) in his book *The Virtual McLuhan* reported that McLuhan was quite familiar with the cybernetics and systems literature.

> McLuhan could almost instantaneously intuit the relevance of Norbert Wiener's and C. E. Shannon and W. Weaver's ideas about cybernetics and systems theory in the light of modernist art, literature, poetics, aesthetic theory and cultural production ... He quickly rejected [Wiener's] mathematical theory of communication, but the impact of the world examined in Wiener's *the Human Use of Human Beings* had a profound effect on McLuhan (ibid. 30).
>
> The ground for recognizing the importance of communication and technology had been prepared by McLuhan's rapid recognition of the significance that Shannon and Weaver's work and Wiener's cybernetics would have on the intellectual world and the necessity of criticizing that approach from the perspective of traditional grammatico-rhetorical theories of communication (ibid. 188).

What I will do in this chapter is to go into greater detail and show how McLuhan incorporated a general systems approach to his treatment of communications, media and the impacts of technology. It is ironic that although McLuhan thought in terms of systems and his methods and insights were systemic, he himself was not systematic in the way in which he organized his written material. Although an avid reader he was not a systematic writer. His insights are scattered throughout his writings. It must be said that he expressed himself more elegantly orally than through his prose. He mostly composed his written texts orally dictating to his wife in the early days of his career and then to his secretary Margaret Stewart for material in which he was the single author. For co-authored works, his partners for the most part took notes and wrote up what they agreed upon in their discussions. They then edited what they had written together with him orally, which is exactly how he and I worked together on the two papers and one book that we co-authored together. From private communication with some of his other co-authors, namely, Eric McLuhan, Harley Parker and Barrington Nevitt, I learned that this is the way they also basically worked with Marshall. McLuhan was a systems thinker, not a systems writer.

What is a Systems Approach?

Before describing how McLuhan's approach to studying media, communications and the impact of technology is a "systems" approach we begin by describing what constitutes a system, and what is the nature of systems thinking and systems theory. A system in the context of systems thinking is a set of interacting components whose impact on each other and the system as a whole is non-linear. It is also the case that a system as a whole has properties that none of its components possess. There are three levels of causal interactions among the system as a whole and its components. These are:

(1) the vertical causal interactions of the top-down interaction of the system as a whole with its components; and
(2) the vertical bottom-up causal interactions of the components of the system with the system as a whole, and finally
(3) the lateral causal interactions of the components of the system with each other.

These three sets of causal interactions cannot be analyzed independently and treated separately. Each set of causal interactions affects the other two. Systems thinking and systems theory takes into account the non-linearity of these three distinct sets of causal interactions. The top-down and bottom up vertical interactions between the system as a whole and its components are non-linear and are affected by the lateral interactions among the components and the lateral interactions are non-linear and they affect and are affected by the vertical ones. In other words, the interactions cannot be disentangled and hence a general systems or ecological approach must be taken to describe such a system. As a result of the complexity of all these interactions, a system, like a living organism for example, have properties that none of its components possess. These properties **emerge** from the **complexity** of the three levels of causality just described. And hence general systems theory sometime goes by the terms, emergence theory or complexity theory. Chaos theory, cybernetics and ecology are also closely related to the general systems approach.

It is therefore not an accident that the general systems approach began in the field of biology where the interactions among living organisms and their environment or umwelt is extremely complex and totally non-linear. This is also the case with the interaction of the organs of an organism and the organism itself. The first to suggest the complexity of these interactions in a comprehensive way was Ludwig von Bertalanffy (1928, 1949, 1968) who coined the term Allgemeine Systemtheorie in his 1949 book, which was translated as General Systems Theory which appears in the title of his 1968 book, *General System Theory: Foundations, Development, Applications*.

McLuhan's General Theory of Media is a General Systems Approach

I claim that McLuhan's General Theory of Media is a general systems approach and hence is an ecological approach given that an ecosystem and a general system are essentially equivalent. The media ecosystem that McLuhan considers parallels Bertalanffy's (1968) general system theory because both involve the non-linear interactions of the components of the system and the system itself. Each element of a general system or a media ecosystem impacts all the other components of the system and the system as a whole and vice-versa each element of the system is impacted by all the other elements of the system and the system as a whole. A general system and a media ecosystem both involve emergent dynamics in which the general system or the media ecosystem has properties that none of its components have.

The first hint of McLuhan embracing a systems approach in his study of media and their effects occurs in a 1955 paper in which McLuhan (1955) wrote: "It is therefore, a simple maxim of communication study that any change in the means of communication will produce a chain of revolutionary consequences at every level of culture and politics. And because of the complexity of the components in this process, predictions and controls are not possible."

McLuhan's description of communication studies is almost a perfect match for a complex general system which has properties that none of its components possess and it is impossible to predict the properties of the general system even if one knows about all the properties of its components in advance. The characteristics of a general system or an ecosystem is that of emergent dynamics by which the components of the general system or the ecosystem interact with each other in a non-linear fashion in which there is both downward, upward and lateral causation between the system and its components. This parallels McLuhan's methodology which he described in the opening line of his book *The Gutenberg Galaxy* where he wrote, "*The Gutenberg Galaxy* develops a mosaic or field approach to its problems. Such a mosaic image of numerous data and quotations in evidence offers the only practical means of revealing causal operations in history (McLuhan 1962, 7)."

Once again in *Understanding Media*, McLuhan (1964, 248) introduces the field notion which he relates to the electric field as described by physicists and uses it to describe electrically configured information and the post-Gutenberg world, which he viewed as "a total field of interacting events in which all men (sic) participate." McLuhan's field approach led to his ecological/environmental way of describing the interaction of all the forms of media with each other and their users. There are just too many elements and interactions to describe them one component at a time in a linear sequential way with the world's population approaching 8 billion people and an even greater number of electronic and digital devices, emails, blogs, Web sites, tweets, videos, podcasts, etc.

McLuhan adopted a "total-field-theory approach," which I believe was influenced by his understanding of modern 20th century science as the following passage suggests, "All types of linear approaches to situations past, present, or future are useless. Already in the sciences there is recognition of the need for a unified field theory, which enable scientists to use one continuous set of terms by way of relating the various scientific universes (McLuhan 1953, 126)."

McLuhan's unified field approach retrieves Einstein's Theory of Relativity in which space and time are united in a four-dimensional space-time continuum. "Using the Laws of Media McLuhan's field approach enhances media ecology, obsolesces content analysis, retrieves Einstein's four-dimensional space-time continuum, and flips into the reversal of cause and effect (Logan 2013, 112–13)."

McLuhan, without explicitly making use of complexity theory and emergent dynamics, was basically applying that kind of thinking to his analysis of communications and the impact of technology that became explicit in the emergence and complexity theories that flourished after McLuhan's passing in 1980. He was aware, however, of the work of Bertalanffy's (1968) with whom he corresponded. It is also the case that they both read each other's work. In an article McLuhan (1955, 107) wrote in 1955 there is a hint of what was to become emergence or complexity theory and certainly a solid application of general systems theory: "It is therefore, a simple maxim of communication study that any change in the means of communication will produce a chain of revolutionary consequences at every level of culture and politics. And because of the complexity of the components in this process, predictions and controls are not possible." Commenting on this passage I wrote:

> I find this 1955 passage quite prescient because one of the basic tenets of complexity theory is that complex non-linear systems have properties not possessed by the components of which they are composed and it is impossible to predict those properties in advance. In terms of biological evolution this translates into the notion that one cannot prestate Darwinian pre-adaptations (Kauffman, Logan et. al. 2007). The reason that I find this prescient is that as early as 1955 way before strong emergence and complexity theory emerged (pun intended), McLuhan seems to be aware of systems theory, which was just beginning to be formulated. It is possible that McLuhan arrived at these ideas on his own as a result of his field approach to understanding media (Logan 2013, 114).

Another indication that McLuhan was thinking in terms of systems theory is this passage from the Hot and Cool Interview with Michael Stearn:

'System' means something to look at. You must have a very high visual gradient to have systemization. In philosophy, before Descartes, there was no 'system.' Plato had no 'system.' Aristotle had no 'system.' My own interest in studying media is a 'systems development' approach. 'Systems Development' is a structural analysis of pressures and strains, the exact opposite of everything that has been meant by 'systems' in the past few centuries ... It is concerned with the inner dynamics of the form (McLuhan 1997a, 74).

Other Examples of McLuhan's General Systems Approach to Media Ecology

In the following section we will describe how many of McLuhan's approaches to understanding media incorporate a general systems approach. McLuhan frequently employs a general systems approach in which the media and their human users become a "general system" àla Bertalanffy's (1968) General System Theory.

From the subtitle of *Understanding Media: Extensions of Man*, McLuhan (1964) is suggesting that media/technologies and humankind form a system that is amenable to a general systems approach. He not only describes the effects of the technology on their human users he also talks about the effects that humans have on their technology when he wrote,

> To behold, use or perceive any extension of ourselves in technological forms is necessarily to embrace it. By continuously embracing technologies, we relate ourselves to them as servo-mechanisms ... Man becomes, as it were, the sex organs of the machine world, as the bee of the plant world, enabling it to fecundate and to evolve ever new forms (ibid., 46).

McLuhan treatment of a figure and its ground merges them into a general system. Given that the subliminal nature of the ground or environment requires an anti-environment to be perceived, the actual general system has three elements: i. the figure; ii. the ground or environment and iii. the anti-environment.

> Any new technology, any extension or amplification of human faculties given material embodiment, tends to create a new environment ... It is in the interplay between the old and new environments that there is generated an innumerable series of problems and confusions ... It is useful to view all the arts and sciences as acting in the role of anti-environments that enable us to perceive the environment (McLuhan 1967a)

> The figure is what appears and the ground is always subliminal. Changes occur in the ground before they occur in the figure. We can project both figure and ground as images of the future using the ground as subplot of subliminal patterns and pressures

and effects which actually come before the more or less final figures to which we normally direct our interest (http://imfpu.blogspot.com/2008/12/magritte.html).

"A new medium is never an addition to an old one, nor does it leave the old one in peace. It never ceases to oppress the older media until it finds new shapes and positions for them (McLuhan 1995, 278)." This last McLuhan quote incorporates the idea that all media and their users become a system. McLuhan's one liner "the user is the content" also incorporates this idea. The medium or technology and their users continually interact with each other. They are part of a Bertalanffian general system (Bertalanffy 1968).

The following quote implies that figure and ground form a general system: "In all patterns, when the ground changes, the figure too is altered by the new interface (McLuhan 1972, 180)." The following passages from McLuhan's Understanding media imply that the whole of humanity together with and because of electric technology form a Bertalanffian general system (Bertalanffy 1968):

> Today, after more than a century of electric technology, we have extended our central nervous system itself in a global embrace, abolishing both space and time as far as our planet is concerned ... In the electric age, when our central nervous system is technologically extended to involve us in the whole of mankind and to incorporate the whole of mankind in us, we necessarily participate, in depth, in the consequences of our every action. It is no longer possible to adopt the aloof and dissociated role of the literate Westerner ... In this electric age we see ourselves being translated more and more into the form of information, moving toward the technological extension of consciousness ... By putting our physical bodies inside our extended nervous systems, by means of electric media, we set up a dynamic by which all previous technologies that are mere extensions of hands and feet and bodily heat-controls - all such extensions of our bodies, including cities - will be translated into information systems (McLuhan 1964, 3, 8 & 57).

Feedforward and the Influence of I. A. Richards on McLuhan

Perhaps McLuhan's first exposure to systems thinking came from his studying with I. A. Richards at Cambridge University where he earned his PhD. I. A. Richards' area of research was rhetoric, which he considered to be more than just the art of persuasion. Richards was concerned with the accuracy of human communication. He considered the field of rhetoric to be about finding remedies for avoiding misunderstandings and hence improving communication as well as understanding how words work. He believed the notion of feedforward was an important tool for achieving these ends. Feedforward is basically a form of pragmatics where pragmatics is the use of context to assist meaning.

The application of feedforward to rhetoric is basically a general systems approach where the system for good communication must not only include the sender, the receiver and the message communicated but the general background to the message which according to Richards must be fed forward. That feedforward provides the context for the message communicated by the sender in order for the receiver to comprehend the full meaning of the sender's message. In other words, Richards claimed that in order to be understood the sender of a message had to feedforward the context of the information.

McLuhan reformulated this idea with his one liner, "the user is the content," meaning that the interpretation of the message sent by the sender is a key component to the meaning of that message. Information is a metaphor that sometimes describes the signal and sometimes the interpretation. The pheromone trails that ants leave are information for the members of their nest, but they are not information for other organisms that might encounter these chemical signals. Without context there can be no information. Signals only become information if the context of the signal has been made clear.

Richards first formally introduced the term feedforward in a paper he presented at the Macy conferees on cybernetics in 1951:

> Perhaps this thing on which I want to put the spotlight will be considered to be included in some ingenious way under the word "feedback." But what I am going to stress stands in an obvious and superficial opposition to "feedback," and it will, in certain frames of thought, be given nearly, if not quite so much, importance, and sometimes more importance than feedback itself in certain connections. It is certainly as circular. You have no doubt fed forward enough to see that what I am going to talk about from now on is feedforward. I am going to try to suggest its importance in describing how language works and, above all, in determining how languages may best be learned (Richards, 1952, p. 54).

The coining of the term feedforward by Richards was no doubt influenced by the term feedback used by cyberneticians and according to the OED was first introduced into the English language in 1920. But as Richards pointed out feedforward stands in superficial opposition to feedback. Feedback is basically reactive whereas feedforward is proactive. Feedforward anticipates where one is headed and sets one's goals. Feedback allows one to see how close one gets to their goals. Richards who stressed the importance of providing the context of what one wanted to communicate might have coined the term feedforward to complement the term feedback used by cyberneticians precisely because the audience that he was addressing at the Macy Conference included the man who coined the term cybernetics, namely Norbert Wiener, as well as other prominent folks in cybernetics including Ludwig von Bertalanffy, Warren McCulloch, Walter Pitts, Claude Shannon, Gregory Bateson, and Heinz von Foerster. The term feedforward as used by Richards suggested that in order to have one's communication understood it was necessary to literally feedforward the context of what one was planning to talk about.

In Marchand's (1989, 32–33 & 36–37) McLuhan biography, Marchand acknowledges the favorable impact on McLuhan of Richards' notion of feedforward. Richard's term feedforward made a big impression on McLuhan. McLuhan wrote to Richards on June 12, 1968 thanking him for mentioning in his book, *So Much Nearer: Essays Towards a World English*, McLuhan's thoughts on the idea of complementarity in quantum mechanics. "I want to mention at once my gratification at your kindly reference to me on page 63 of So Much Nearer. Naturally, I owe you an enormous debt since Cambridge days." Towards the end of the letter McLuhan writes, "Your wonderful word 'feedforward' suggests to me the principle of the probe, the technique of the 'suspended judgment,' which has been called the greatest discovery of the 20th century (Molinaro, C. McLuhan, and Toye 1987, 355)."

McLuhan made explicit use of the term feedforward in the title of his book *War and Peace in the Global Village: An Inventory of Some of the Current Spastic Situations That Could be Eliminated by More Feedforward* (McLuhan and Fiore 1968, bolding mine). He also used the term feedforward (bolded) in following six excerpts from his writings:

> Computers offer the potential of instantaneous translation of any code or language into any other code or language. If a data feedback is possible through the computer, why not a **feedforward** of thought whereby a world consciousness links into a world computer? Via the computer, we could logically proceed from translating languages to bypassing them entirely in favor of an integral cosmic unconsciousness somewhat similar to the collective unconscious envisioned by Bergson. The computer thus holds out the promise of a technologically engendered state of universal understanding and unity, a state of absorption in the logos that could knit mankind into one family and create a perpetuity of collective harmony and peace. This is the real use of the computer, not to expedite marketing or solve technical problems but to speed the process of discovery and orchestrate terrestrial — and eventually galactic — environments and energies (McLuhan 1969a).

> Poets and artists live on frontiers. They have no feedback, only **feedforward** (McLuhan 1970c, 44).

> The technique of cliché-as-probe, by contrast, 'is always at the "interface" of discourse': **'feed[ing]-forward** … but always engaged in retrieving old clichés from every sphere of human activity' (McLuhan and Watson 1970, 164).
>
> But in the past century it has come generally acknowledged that, in the words of Wyndham Lewis. "The artist is always engaged in writing a detailed history of the future because he is the only person aware of the nature of the present" (McLuhan 1964, 70).
>
> Electronic man becomes a hunter, a prober once more. He begins to live by **"feedforward,"** not "feedback" (McLuhan 1968).
>
> At instant speeds in our resonant Echoland, it is fatal to "wait and see". Feedback relying on experience is now too slow. We must know in advance of action. The **"feedforward"** of knowledge based on **pattern recognition** of process is essential for reprogramming beyond ideologies. What had always appeared inevitable can thus be bypassed (McLuhan 1995, 77).

The last item in the above list of McLuhan's mention of feedforward suggests that feedforward is based on pattern recognition, which is an important element of McLuhan's GToM. Long before the take off of complexity theory with the founding of the Santa Fe Institute in 1984 McLuhan was already incorporating many of the ideas that became part of complexity theory in his work dating back to the 1960s such as his focus on pattern recognition. "We are now living in a world where things change so rapidly that anybody can spot the configuration, the pattern of change and we're living increasingly in a world of pattern recognition (https://www.themediumisthemassage.com/the-film/, accessed May 22, 2021)."

McLuhan's stress on pattern recognition is an integral part of complexity theory. McLuhan's field approach and his rejection of a linear sequential, mechanistic, one thing at a time approach translates into the anti-reductionist stance that is at the heart of complexity theory's focus on non-linear dynamics. McLuhan opposed the reductionism of what Blake called the "single vision" of Newton. With his co-author Barrington Nevitt he embraced the notion that the dynamics of media in the age of electric communication is non-linear. They wrote,

> Nils Bohr's complementarity that represents 'atomic' interactions as both 'acoustic' waves and 'visual' particles is exemplified by every process involving the continuous interplay of simultaneous actions …. Such complementarity of figure-ground appears as a causal relation in all 'pre-packaged' processes. Complementarity is the process whereby effects become causes. Today, as causes and effects merge instantaneously, the new common ground is neither container nor category, but the vastness of space via media (McLuhan and Nevitt 1972).

B. W. Powe (2014, 231) used the term **feedforward** describing McLuhan's notion of communication when he wrote, "McLuhan insisted that communication was not mere transmission, agency from one point to another. It is participation and feedback, echoing and reverberation. It is **feedforward**: probe and propulsion into response and revision, into remaking and extension."

The Systems Approach of the Media Ecology Community

The general systems approach of McLuhan no doubt had an influence on the practitioners of media ecology. In this section we review the way in which a number of media ecologists have incorporated the general systems approach in their media ecology analyzes. We begin with Lance Strate (2017) and his book *Media Ecology: An Approach to Understanding the Human Condition*. Strate focuses specifically on the general systems approach in section 7.6 Systems and Emergence where he demonstrates that media ecology incorporates a systems approach. He also identifies media ecologists that have adopted a systems approach. In particular he mentions Christine Nystrom and Neil Postman, the founder of the media ecology program at NYU with whom he studied and where he earned his PhD. Strate emphasizes the connection between ecology including media ecology and systems thinking by quoting Postman (1992, 18) who wrote: "Technological change is neither additive nor subtractive. It is ecological. I mean 'ecological' in the same sense as the word is used by environmental scientists. One significant change generates total change ... This is how the ecology of media works as well. A new technology does not add or subtract something. It changes everything." Postman's last remark "it changes everything" parallels McLuhan's observation that we quoted above, "A new medium is never an addition to an old one, nor does it leave the old one in peace (McLuhan 1995, 278)."

Strate (2017, 21) identifies other media ecologists who like him see a connection between media ecology and systems theory including your author: "Nystrom's (1973) treatise on media ecology is also concerned with systems theory, Logan (2013, 2016) argues that McLuhan utilized systems theory in his approach to understanding media, and a systems orientation informs the work of Meyrowitz (1985), Ong (1977), and Postman (1976, 1979, 2006)."

Islas and Bernal (2016, 190) argue in an essay entitled Media Ecology: A Complex and Systemic Metadiscipline, as their title indicates, that there is a close connection between media ecology and systems theory. They define media ecology as "a complex and systemic metadiscipline whose object of study is the changes and effects that have occurred in society as a result of the evolution of technology and media throughout history."

One of the earliest media ecologists to see the parallel between media ecology and systems thinking was Joshua Meyrowitz (1985, 339, bolding is the authors) although he did not use the term media ecology but spoke of the "media matrix," which he defines in the following terms: "It is a fiction to discuss any one medium or type of medium in isolation. The media interact with each other within what might be called the **media matrix**-the interlocking network of all coexistent media." He also introduces the notion of "effect loops" in Chapter 11 with their systemic impacts on social change brought about by new technologies.

Meyrowitz (ibid., 19) links the "media matrix" or media ecology, if you will, to systems theory: "There is a clear analogy here to the industrialization of society, which had a great impact on social organization and labor, and ended 'agricultural' forms of society, but without destroying our fundamental dependence on the production of food. The important underlying principle is firmly rooted in systems theory and ecology."

Conclusion

McLuhan's deployment of general systems thinking have changed the entire way in which the field of communications and the study of the impact of technology have changed. In Chapter Two we described the 10 elements of McLuhan's General Theory of Media (GToM). In this the concluding section of Chapter Five we show how each of these 10 elements arose in some way as a result of McLuhan's systems approach:

Probes: rather than working from a theory of communications McLuhan adopted a general systems approach and probed the impact of communication media and other technologies on their users.

Figure/ground, the key element in McLuhan's general theory of media: McLuhan assumed that every figure and the ground (or the environment) in which it operated formed a general system. One could not understand a figure unless one took the ground which it created and in which it operated into account.

The medium is the message: the content of a medium and the medium itself form a general system. The medium changes the way in which the content is perceived. A Shakespearian play that appears as a script, acted out in a theater or is used to make a movie or that is read silently or out loud are completely different although the content in terms of the words of the play are the same. The content, on the other hand, can change the way in which a medium is perceived. A movie that is a thriller, an action film or a romantic comedy will each change the way in which the medium of the movie is perceived.

The subliminal nature of the ground of a medium is revealed by the creation of an anti-environment: the anti-environment that reveals the ground or environment, the ground or environment itself and the figure that operates in the environment form a general system in which each element of the triad interacts with the other two elements.

The reversal of cause and effect: the evolution of technology operates such that the effect of a new technology becomes the cause of some newer technology. The effect of the telegraph became the cause of the telephone and the effect the mainframe computer became the cause of the personal computer, which in turn became the cause or enabled word processing, the modem, the tablet, the smartphone, the Internet, the Web, and Amazon. Each effect becomes a niche in which a new figure emerges. The reversal of cause and effects is typical in a general system because of the non-linearity of the causal connections.

The importance of percept over concept, the human sensorium and media as extensions of man (sic): the effects of media are perceived and causes are conceived. Since there is a reversal of cause and effects it follows there is also a reversal of concepts and percepts.

Communication in the oral, written, and electric ages; acoustic and visual space: the three modes of communication of oral, written and electric form a general system that interact with each other. The content of a new medium is an older medium. The content of writing is speech and the content of electric media are speech and writing.

The Global Village: the notion of the global village considers the planet and the electric media that connect it as a general system.

Media as environments and media ecology: media ecology is systems thinking approach for understanding media.

The Laws of Media: The Laws of Media is a general system approach that ties together past, present and future: the past through obsolescence and retrieval, the present through enhancement and the future through reversal.

References

Bertalanffy, Ludwig von. *Kritische Theorie der Formbildung*. Berlin: Gebrüder Borntraeger, 1928.

Bertalanffy, Ludwig von. "Zu einer allgemeinen Systemlehre." *Blätter für deutsche Philosophie* 3/4 (1945): 31–45.

Bertalanffy, Ludwig von. *General System Theory: Foundations, Development, Applications*. New York: George Braziller, revised edition 1976, 1968.

Islas, Octavio, and Juan David Bernal. "Media Ecology: A Complex and Systemic Metadiscipline." *MDPI Philosophies* 1, no. 3 (2016): 190–98.

Kauffman, Stuart, Robert K. Logan, Robert Este, Randy Goebel, David Hobill, and Ilya Smulevich. "Propagating Organization: An Inquiry." *Biology and Philosophy* 23 (2007): 27–45.

Logan, Robert K. *McLuhan Misunderstood: Setting the Record Straight*. Toronto: The Key Publishing House, 2013.

Marchand, Philip. *Marshall McLuhan: The Medium and the Messenger*. Toronto: Random House, 1989.

McLuhan, Marshall. "Not for Children". *Exploration* 1 (1953): 117–27.

McLuhan, Marshall. "Communication and Communication Art: A Historical Approach to the Media." *Teachers College Record* 57, no. 2 (1955): 104–10.

McLuhan, Marshall. *The Gutenberg Galaxy: The Making of Typographic Man*. Toronto: University of Toronto Press, 1962.

McLuhan, Marshall. *Understanding Media: Extensions of Man*. New York: McGraw Hill, 1964. (The page references in the text are for the McGraw Hill paperback second edition. Readers should be aware that the pagination in other editions is different.)

McLuhan, Marshall. "Casting my Perils before Swains." In *McLuhan Hot and Cool*, edited by Gerard Emanuel Stearn. New York: Dial Press, 1967.

McLuhan, Marshall. "Include Me Out: The Reversal of the Overheated Image." *Playboy* 15, no. 12 (December, 1968): 61–64, 245.

McLuhan, Marshall. Playboy Magazine Interview. *Playboy* 16, no. 3 (March, 1969): 53–74, 158.

McLuhan, Marshall. *Culture Is Our Business*. New York and Toronto: McGraw-Hill, 1970.

McLuhan, Marshall. "The Future of the Book." In *Understanding Me: Lectures & Interviews*, edited by Stephanie McLuhan & David Staines. Toronto: McClelland & Stewart, 1972.

McLuhan, Marshall. "Media as They Affect Media." In *Essential McLuhan*, edited by Eric McLuhan and Frank Zingrone. Concord, ON: Anansi, 1995.

McLuhan, Marshall. "The Hot and Cool Interview." In *Media Research: Technology, Art and Communication*, edited by Michael Moos, 45–78. Abington, UK: Routledge, 1997.

McLuhan, Marshall, and Quentin Fiore. *War and Peace in the Global Village*. New York: Simon & Shuster, 1968.

McLuhan, Marshall, and Wilfred Watson. *From Cliché to Archetype*. New York: The Viking Press, 1970.

McLuhan, Marshall, and Barrington Nevitt. *Take Today: The Executive as Dropout*. Toronto: Longman Canada, 1972.

Meyrowitz, Joshua. *No Sense of Place: The Impact of Electronic Media on Social Behavior*. New York: Oxford University Press, 1985.

Molinaro, Matie, Corrine McLuhan, and William Toye (eds). *Letters of Marshall McLuhan*. Toronto: Oxford University Press, 1987.

Nystrom, Christine. Towards a Science of Media Ecology: The Formulation of Integrated Conceptual Paradigms for the Study of Human Communication Systems. (Unpublished doctoral dissertation), 1973.
Ong, Walter. *Interfaces of the Word.* Ithica, NY: Cornell University Press, 1977.
Postman, Neil. *Crazy Talk, Stupid Talk.* New York: Delacorte, 1976.
Postman, Neil. *Teaching as a Conserving Activity.* New York: Delacorte, 1979.
Postman, Neil. *Technopoly: The Surrender of Culture to Technology.* New York: Alfred A. Knopf, 1992.
Postman, Neil. "Media Ecology Education." *Explorations in Media Ecology* 5, no. 1 (2006): 5–14.
Powe, Bruce W. *Marshall McLuhan and Northrop Frye: Apocalypse and Alchemy.* Toronto: University of Toronto Press, 2014.
Richards, I. A. "Communication Between Men: The Meaning of Language." In *Transactions of 8th Macy Conference – Cybernetics: Circular Causal and Feedback Mechanisms in Biological and Social Systems*, edited by Heinz Foerster. New York: Josiah Macy, Jr. Foundation, 1952.
Strate, Lance. *Media Ecology: An Approach to Understanding the Human Condition.* New York: Peter Lang Publishing, 2017.
Theall, Donald. *The Virtual Marshall McLuhan.* Montreal & Kingston: McGill-Queen's University Press, 2001.

CHAPTER SIX

Cataloguing McLuhan Reversals

Introduction

This chapter is a catalogue of McLuhan reversals based on his writings and his observations of the oral, written and electric ages of communication. In addition, it also contains a projection of what his reversals might have been if he had survived into the digital age, which sadly he did not. The purpose of this chapter is to collect all of McLuhan's reversals and McLuhan-like reversals in one place to support the hypothesis that thinking in terms of reversals was an integral part of McLuhan's approach to understanding media and their impacts and is also a useful tool for understanding the digital technologies that he never had a chance to experience.

McLuhan's reversals have been divided into 3 categories based on his writings and a 4th category has been added, namely McLuhan-like reversals for the digital age:

1. reversals that were part of McLuhan's methodology as used in his General Theory of Media;
2. reversals that are associated with the transition from the age of oral communication to the age of written communication and mechanical forms;
3. reversals that are associated with the transition from the age of written communication and mechanical forms to electric forms of communication; and

4. reversals that are associated with the transition from the age of electric forms of communication to digital age of communication formulated in the spirit of McLuhan reversals

Catalogue of McLuhan's Use of Reversals in His Methodology

figure reverses into ground or environment;
percept reverses into concept;
cause reverses into effect;
environment reverses into anti-environment
media reverse into extensions of man
extensions of man reverse into amputations
media reverse into environments
medium reverses into massage
environments as passive wrapping reverse into environments as active processes
a medium pushed too far reverses into complementary or opposite form;
a work of art or performance reverses into the public or audience;
content reverses into user ("the user is the content")
exposition reverses into exploration;
service of media reverses into disservice of media;
patterns of technology use reverses into patterns of societal organization;
obsolesced technology reverses into an art form;
invention reverses into mother of necessity;
user of a medium reverses into servomechanism of that medium;
jokes reverse into grievances;
content or message reverses into the medium ("the medium is the message");
communication as the
transmission of information reverses into communication as
participation in a common experience

Reversals from Oral Age to the Age of Written Communication

ear reverses into eye;
oral reverses into literate;
acoustic space reverses into visual space;

bard reverses into scribe
poetry reverses into prose
Homer reverses into written history as in Thucydides;
Eric Havelocks's tribal encyclopedia reverses into codified law;
tribe reverses into city state
tallies reverse into numeric notation
apprenticeship learning reverses into formal education;

Reversals from the Age of Written Communication and Mechanical Forms to the Age of Electric Communication and Forms

the literate reverses into the electric;
mechanical technology reverses into electric technology;
patterns of written communication reverse into patterns of oral communication;
visual space reverses into acoustic space;
the written page reverses into the movie and TV screen
linear causal connections reverse into a field or ecological approach;
consumers reverse into producers;
the age of manufactured goods reverses into the age of 'do it yourself';
automation reverses into do it yourself
DIY as home improvements reverses into DIY as a culture;
goal-seeking or job reverses into role-playing;
centralism reverses into decentralism;
specialism and expertise reverses into interdisciplinarity;
expert reverses into group discovery and the task force;
individual effort reverses into task force;
monopolies of knowledge reverses into crowd sourcing;
linear sequential mechanical ordering reverses into instantaneity and all-at-onceness;
fragmentation, specialization reverses into wholeness, diversity, involvement;
separation of function reverses into integrated and organic integration
detachment reverses into involvement
Eastern cultural forms reverse into Western cultural forms;
Western cultural forms reverse into Eastern cultural forms;
country side reverses into the city as focus of commerce;
city reverses into countryside as place of leisure;
joke reverses into one-liner;

classification reverses into pattern recognition;
fixed point of view reverses into interface and pattern
connection reverses into pattern;
answers reverse into questions in education;
hardware reverses into software;
mechanical forms reverse into electronic forms;
explosion reverses into implosion;
local culture reverses into universal global culture;
city forms reverse into highway forms;
highway form reverses into city form
in modern industry the artist reverses from the ivory tower to the control tower
industrial labor reverses into learning as a paid occupation
Three McLuhan predictions
mainframe computers reverse into personal computers (a prediction);
products reverse into services (a prediction);
printed book as a product reverses into books as a service (a prediction);

Reversals in the Digital Age

With the exception of the **reversal of electric mass media into the digital media** the reversals of the digital age are the same as those in the electric age. All of the above reversals for electric media apply for digital media. However, some of the reversals in the digital age are different in character because they are more pronounced. We list here each of these reversals that are more pronounced. We indicate for each of these (in parentheses) in what sense they differ from the same reversal in the electric age.

pattern of digital communication reverses into pattern of oral communication;
(Internet-based writing such as email and texting have a more pronounced oral characteristic to them.)
visual space reverses into acoustic space;
(The Internet facilitates the arrival of information on a global scale. Smart phone users are bombarded on all sides from a variety of electronic messages unlike the viewers of TV and the listeners of radio.)
linear causal connection reverses into a field or ecological approach;
(In the digital age there is the addition feature that the field elements are interconnected by the Internet and other forms of networking.)
consumer reverses into producer;
age of manufactured goods reverses into the age of "do it yourself";

automation reverses into do it yourself;
DIY as home improvements reverses into DIY as a culture;
(There are more "do it yourself" options available in the digital age than the electric age such as: self-publishing, making things using 3D printing. In addition, because of the two-way flow of information with the Internet users can create their own artistic or journalistic creations and find audiences using such outlets as personalized Web sites, blogs, podcasts, and postings on YouTube, Vimeo, and social media such as Facebook, Instagram, Snapchat, Twitter, Reddit and TikTok.)
goal-seeking or job reverses into role-playing;
(Many more folks are self-employed using the Net and the Web as a platform to earn a living or start a business online.)
centralism reverses into decentralism;
(The Internet and the Web are totally decentralized. With personal computers and smart phones connected to the Internet users are at the center of a global flow of information that they can access from almost any place on the planet. In addition, because of the two-way flow of information that the Internet facilitates they can also get their message out anywhere they find themselves.)
specialism and expertise reverses into interdisciplinarity;
(The reversal from specialism and expertise into interdisciplinarity because of the ease of access to information and collaborators. The reporting of research is not so siloed because of the Internet.)
expert reverses into group discovery and the task force;
(The Internet facilitates collaboration on a global scale.)
individual effort reverses into task force;
(more so in the digital age because of the ease of access to collaborators using the Internet)
monopolies of knowledge reverses into crowd sourcing;
(The Internet facilitates accessing the knowledge of others on a global scale.)
linear sequential mechanical ordering reverses into instantaneity and all-at-onceness;
(the transmission of information speeds up with digital media and hence things are even more instantaneous and all-at-once.)
Eastern cultural forms reverse into Western cultural forms;
Western cultural forms reverse into Eastern cultural forms;
(Cultural exchanges increase through the use of digital technologies that facilitate communication on a global level.)
mainframes reverse into personal computers [a McLuhan prediction] products reverse into services [a McLuhan prediction];

printed book as a product reverses into a service [a McLuhan prediction];
(McLuhan's predictions from the electric age were realized in the digital age for all three of these developments with e-book as the format in which the printed book becomes a service.)
hardware reverses into software [a McLuhan prediction]
(This is what literally happened in the digital age)
explosion reverses into implosion;
(all forms of human knowledge and expression implode on the Internet)
local culture reverses into universal global culture.
(The Internet facilitates cultural exchanges and hence facilitates the creation of a universal global culture)

Lance Strate
General Editor

This series is devoted to scholarship relating to media ecology, a field of inquiry defined as the study of media as environments. Within this field, the term "medium" can be defined broadly to refer to any human technology or technique, code or symbol system, invention or innovation, system or environment. Media ecology scholarship typically focuses on how technology, media, and symbolic form relate to communication, consciousness, and culture, past, present and future. This series is looking to publish research that furthers the formal development of media ecology as a field; that brings a media ecology approach to bear on specific topics of interest, including research and theoretical or philosophical investigations concerning the nature and effects of media or a specific medium; that includes studies of new and emerging technologies and the contemporary media environment as well as historical studies of media, technology, and modes and codes of communication; scholarship regarding technique and the technological society; scholarship on specific types of media and culture (e.g., oral and literate cultures, image, etc.), or of specific aspects of culture such as religion, politics, education, journalism, etc.; critical analyses of art and popular culture; and studies of how physical and symbolic environments function as media.

For additional information about this series or for the submission of manuscripts, please contact:
  Lance Strate, Series Editor | *strate@fordham.edu*

To order other books in this series, please contact our Customer Service Department:
  peterlang@presswarehouse.com (within the U.S.)
  orders@peterlang.com (outside the U.S.)

Or browse online by series:
  www.peterlang.com

www.ingramcontent.com/pod-product-compliance
Lightning Source LLC
Chambersburg PA
CBHW050123020526
44112CB00035B/2369